PRAISE FOR *HERE, NOW*

"If you're in the mood to sit down for coffee with a friend who is not only hilarious, but so wise and gut-wrenchingly honest, this book will do the trick. My friend Kate Merrick has uncovered the secrets to live a more present and intentional life, and we are all blessed that she is willing to share. Put *Here, Now* on your reading list."

—Esther Fleece Allen, SPEAKER AND
AUTHOR OF *NO MORE FAKING FINE*

"I love the simplicity yet powerful message behind *Here, Now*. Kate's writing style is so relatable and has truly opened my eyes to becoming more present and enjoying God's gifts that we encounter every single day. This book reminds us that the best things in life are not behind a screen or on social media, rather they are enjoying the world, people, and cultures for what they truly are. It is an uplifting reminder to laugh, cry, be silly, and experience the realness of life."

—Lakey Peterson, PROFESSIONAL SURFER

"*Here, Now* is like a refreshing breeze of sage advice from a lifelong friend you've been in the foxhole with. Kate graciously brings you into her story while encouraging you to slow down and take in the scenery of your own. Whether on the mountaintop, in the trenches, or somewhere in the vast distance between, it's a reminder to pump the brakes and feast on the landscape the Artist is painting on your life's canvas—something we need to hear daily."

—Kaimana Plemer, CREATOR OF HE>I

"I didn't realize it, but I have been waiting for this book. I've been waiting for permission to opt out of the noise that I keep innocently inviting in and get tired of trying to shout over. I'm so grateful for Kate's story, for her encouragement, for her testimony. I have been living wrong, making poor choices, and gravitating toward a false sense of connection. I am craving a life that is rich and a life that is real. *Here, Now* is a beautiful and poignant guidepost pointing me toward that realness and richness I so long for."

—Lindsey Nobles, Onsite Workshops

"*Here, Now* may be the most important book you read this year. Timely, relevant, convicting, yet full of humor and grace, Kate speaks to the heart of the issues we all wrestle with, whether we talk about it or not. Sharing the intimate journey that has brought Kate and her family to where they are today, this book is an absolute gift to the world—a treasure not to be taken lightly. Kate lives this message every day, and after reading her book I think we all might find ourselves moving towards a less distracted and more present life."

—Monica Swanson, blogger and author of *Boy Mom*

"Equal parts inspiring and convicting, Kate skillfully shares hard-won wisdom and beautiful lessons of faith, courage, and perspective. Readers are invited to take stock and evaluate the true essentials of life. Down to earth, relatable, fun, and challenging, I found myself encouraged rather than shamed as I considered my choices and interactions in our tech-saturated world. This timely and relevant book is full of stories of hope and grace. Halfway through the book I deleted a time-wasting game off my phone. Rather than numbing out and unhealthy escaping, I felt motivated to seek more meaningful connection here and now. Kate's love for God and for the people blessed to know her shines through every page. Two hearty thumbs up!"

—Vivian Mabuni, speaker and author of *Warrior in Pink* and *Open Hands, Willing Heart*

"Reading *Here, Now* is like putting on glasses for the first time after failing an eye exam. Kate helps us see in a fresh way what really matters in life, what deserves our time and attention, and conversely, what does not. But what I like the most about this book is that it doesn't just pitch a tent in the showing, it also gets to the hard work of choosing and doing. Living a courageous, intentional life, free of unnecessary distraction marks the life of Kate Merrick, and she invites us into that same story of life and freedom."

—Krista Gilbert, AUTHOR OF *RECLAIMING HOME* AND
COHOST OF THE OPEN DOOR SISTERHOOD PODCAST

"*Here, Now* is the ideal book for the present day faith pioneer. Kate's wise nuggets of truth and call to savor the moments in front of us are woven with intention, grace, and biblical encouragement that the very best life God has for us is the one unplugged and present to. I offer a confident high five and all the yeses to *Here, Now*!"

—Bekah Pogue, AUTHOR OF *CHOOSING REAL*, LISTENER,
PASTURE FOUNDER, SPIRITUAL-DIRECTOR-IN-TRAINING,
AND A HUGE FAN OF WOMEN ON THE FRINGE

"From the very first sentence of *Here, Now* I was hooked. Every page is filled with the unique combination of Kate's effervescent personality and her hard-earned wisdom from a life well fought for. This is a must-read for anyone who doesn't want to miss what God has for them, no matter the circumstances. A guidebook for those who want to see, hear, taste, smell, and feel the world in all of its beauty and pain with Kate as the ultimate guide. You do not want to miss this book."

—Alexandra Kuykendall, AUTHOR OF *LOVING MY ACTUAL
LIFE* AND COFOUNDER OF THE OPEN DOOR SISTERHOOD

"The digital age has given us instant accessibility and a sense of connectedness far and wide but has left a generation thirsty for more than the shallows. Kate Merrick's voice sings prophetic to those who long for the deep. In *Here, Now* she not only leads readers into the gift of how to be fully awake to their real flesh and blood lives, but also to the everyday holy presence of God as a legacy to embrace and impart."

—Kristen Kill, AUTHOR OF *FINDING SELAH*

"Presence isn't a gender issue. Men often escape into work, sports, fantasy, or living vicariously through entertainment and social feeds. Through poetic grace and humility, Kate returns us to the joy of living our real, best, and only life. It's Kate's wisdom that guides us through the greatest personal challenge of our day, but it's the beauty of her writing that opens our hearts to hear it."

—Roger W. Thompson, AUTHOR, WOODWORKER,
AND FLY FISHERMAN

"Kate describes with clarity and compassion the 'overcrowded life.' A life I so desperately need a break from. Since Kate and I are friends, I can say with confidence she embodies the wise and liberating rhythms she describes in *Here, Now*. Rhythms that recenter our lives on Jesus and wholeheartedly embrace the peace and joy he offers to us in the midst of chaos."

—Kat Armstrong, COFOUNDER OF POLISHED, SPEAKER,
AND AUTHOR OF *NO MORE HOLDING BACK*

"Kate has developed the superpower of being fully present in every moment. And, thankfully, she is sharing that power with us in *Here, Now*. Her book was just what I needed in this season of my life, and I highly recommend it! I believe it will transform the way women (and men!) live their lives—more fully present in our *here, now*."

—Renee Swope, BESTSELLING AUTHOR OF *A CONFIDENT HEART*
AND FORMER RADIO COHOST OF PROVERBS 31 MINISTRIES

here
now

UNEARTHING PEACE AND PRESENCE
IN AN OVERCONNECTED WORLD

KATE MERRICK

NELSON
BOOKS

An Imprint of Thomas Nelson

Published in Nashville, Tennessee, by Nelson Books, an imprint of Thomas Nelson. Nelson Books and Thomas Nelson are registered trademarks of HarperCollins Christian Publishing, Inc.

Published in association with the literary agency of D. C. Jacobson & Associates, LLC, an Author Management Company, www.dcjacobson.com.

Thomas Nelson titles may be purchased in bulk for educational, business, fund-raising, or sales promotional use. For information, please e-mail SpecialMarkets@ThomasNelson.com.

Scripture quotations are taken from the Holy Bible, New Living Translation. © 1996, 2004, 2007, 2013, 2015 by Tyndale House Foundation. Used by permission of Tyndale House Publishers, Inc., Carol Stream, Illinois 60188. All rights reserved.

Any Internet addresses, phone numbers, or company or product information printed in this book are offered as a resource and are not intended in any way to be or to imply an endorsement by Thomas Nelson, nor does Thomas Nelson vouch for the existence, content, or services of these sites, phone numbers, companies, or products beyond the life of this book.

ISBN 978-0-7180-9282-5 (TP)
ISBN 978-0-7180-9312-9 (eBook)

Library of Congress Control Number: 2018957868

Printed in the United States of America
19 20 21 22 23 LSC 10 9 8 7 6 5 4 3 2 1

To Isaiah:
From the first moment I saw your face, I knew I didn't want to miss a thing. You have filled my last eighteen years with awesome. You are strong, humble, kind, brave, hilarious, and I love watching you build a beautiful life, one moment at a time. Also, no one rocks Israel like you. I love you, bro-bro.

CONTENTS

FOREWORD

I'll never forget the day I met Kate. We were both at a conference, and when I spotted her name on the speaker lineup, it rang a bell because multiple people had said to me over the past few months, "Jamie, you *have* to get Kate Merrick on your podcast." They told me that not only was she awesome, but her story was incredible, she loved God a whole lot, and we would become fast friends. They were right about all of those things.

We finally got our moment to talk at a restaurant after the conference. We squeezed into a booth and entered into one of the most intimate and special conversations I have ever had the privilege to be a part of. I didn't know it was going to be so special or I definitely would have approached her sooner—maybe backstage where it wasn't so loud or at a coffee shop where we could have lingered for hours over lattes. But that's not what God had planned.

In those precious moments, Kate invited me into the

pain of losing her daughter to cancer a few years earlier. It's an invitation that I could tell wasn't just thrown around. I listened to every word that poured from her lips. I wept with her and for her. I hugged her when all of my words failed me. And that's all I will tell you of our conversation, because when something feels so sacred and special, you hold it tight—close to your heart.

Kate taught me something that night (and throughout our friendship she continues to teach me), life is short and we get to choose how we face it. Did you read that correctly? Not that life is short and we get to choose how it goes, but that life is *short* and we get to choose *how we face it*. We are in control of our emotions, our attitudes, and our diligence toward our life, even when our circumstances seem out of control. (Side note: our circumstances are always out of our control. There's one Guy controlling them all, and it's not you. Sorry to break that news to you, if you didn't already know!)

One of the things that has struck me the most about Kate is how she removed herself from an online world while cancer was taking her daughter's life and her family was begging God to make it stop, and she entered into her real world with all of her might—her real world where she was asking God to heal her daughter's body and not take her home just yet—pleading with God to remove the sickness and create healthy cells. That night, squeezed together in our booth, Kate told me that it was then that she decided to quit showcasing her life for everyone to see and to start living her life for God, her family, and herself.

If you are anything like me, that makes you stop and think about your own life. How are you and I living our lives? Are we moving so quickly from one thing to the next that we are missing beautiful, sacred, and special moments? Are we more concerned with getting the perfect filter on a picture to show the world our special moments than we are about putting our phones down and actually living those moments?

If we are honest, I would bet that more often than not, we are missing the moments. We're living for the camera, for the likes, for the next big event. What my friend Kate has done for me as a friend—and what she can do for you through this book—is draw me in and remind me that I do get to pick how I face my life. You do too. You get to pick how you show up in circumstances and moments in your everyday world. Kate's decision years ago to be present with the people who were right in front of her over being present with people through a screen and social media has altered her intentionality in all of her relationships. Her diligence toward life shines through in this book and my hope for you, dear friend, as you read this, is that you will take a look at your own life through a new lens—a lens of hope and intentionality, a lens of contentment and joy. You don't have to walk through cancer for this new outlook on life. You just need to change the way that you view your world right now.

Your current circumstances do hold something beautiful—you just might need a new lens. When you and I do this, what we will see is the beauty of God all around us, no matter what life is throwing at us at the moment. Slow down, take in your life, find the beauty, and see God moving all around you—it's worth it.

Jamie Ivey, bestselling author of *If You Only Knew*, host of *The Happy Hour with Jamie Ivey* podcast, and fan of Kate Merrick *one*

A COLLECTION OF MOMENTS

There are no holier experiences on this earth than birth and death, those astonishing moments when souls arrive and when they leave. The coming is the "hello, world" loved ones were waiting for with eyes wide and fists clenched, when brand-new lungs fill to the last alveolus with the sudden inflation of oxygen. When the cries are lusty and heartbreakingly beautiful. The going, on the other hand, is the "goodbye, world" loved ones wished would never happen, when worn-out lungs softly sigh their last goodbye, as the organic releases to the supernatural. It's the heartbreakingly beautiful hush of passing through the veil, as those dearest watch with furrowed brows, and yet this time, with open hands. Hello and goodbye. Just like that.

There's a lot that happens in between those moments, between arms filled with hello-love and arms empty with goodbye-love. A lot. We tend to focus on the beginning and the end, but it's the collection of all the in-between moments that actually make up a life, a whole God-given, genuine life. One that starts with wide-open possibility, with a clean slate, with adventure ahead and heartbreak on the horizon. Each moment builds upon the other, slowly revealing who we become, revealing the returns of what we have chosen to invest in. Each moment sowing into the whole, whether they are exciting and joyful, boring and burdensome, or painful and steeped in sorrow. Each moment counts, from start to finish, from first inhale to last sigh.

How easy it is to sit behind my computer screen and say how much each moment matters while finding, if I'm honest, the in-between part to be a tad distasteful. Too often I'm steeped in discontentment with the business of life, dissatisfied with how the chips are falling. The impulse is to fast-forward through the uglier, tiresome, and tedious bits in life. *Gloss over the tough spots. Don't dwell too much on the precious parts. Don't feel too much. Keep life at bay. Check off the to-do list.* I allow life to become mechanical, obligatory, unscented, and then wonder why I'm so dissatisfied, why contentment is a struggle.

But there is so much to lean into between those first and last breaths: raw beauty and abysmal pain, rapturous joy and acute sorrow, wearying work and life-giving play. Mortal monotony and sacred splendor. I know it's there, yet I smooth right over it, attempting to glide through on my own terms. I label the fragments of a life as *good* or *bad*, trying to keep them separate from each other, passing judgment on whether I want to show up for them or not.

As if I have a choice.

The night before my daughter Daisy was diagnosed

for the first time, it was business as usual. Kids tucked in, dishes clean and neatly stacked. Laundry passed from washer to dryer, steadily humming the soundtrack of the American family. Relaxed and tired, I lay in bed, shopping for some tinted moisturizer from Sephora, hemming and hawing over the million different options. I had expectations of normalcy as I lay there, blithely wondering if I should go with the nontoxic brand or the one with the microscopic sparkles. Both promised to make my freckled thirty-four-year-old skin dewy, irresistible. I spent almost an hour on that website, completely unaware that just sixteen hours later, my life as I knew it would take a sharp turn.

The minutes ticked by, spilling out of my fingers onto the computer keyboard. They rolled to the floor and down the hall, slipped underneath my front door and into the storm drain that leads to the ocean. Moments that were more valuable than I knew. Poured out, wasted. I would never get them back.

I couldn't have known what was coming, of course. There was no way. And if I did know, I'm not sure what I'd have been doing instead. Perhaps I'd be praying, maybe spending serious quality time with my husband, Britt. Maybe I would still be buying the makeup, but I certainly wouldn't have spent forty-five minutes on it. Get in, get out. No need to scroll. No need to squander even the briefest of moments. Not every second of life can be magical, but we need not waste time. Still, that is our way, is it not? Tune out. Treat time as if it's endless and we can have as much of it as we want.

As the story goes, the next day Daisy fell down at school, went to the hospital, and was given a truckload of morphine and a cancer diagnosis. We moved in to the hospital, we held our breaths, we prayed hard through surgery. Around the clock, we suffered constant intrusion from residents, nurses, doctors, lab techs, admin people, and social workers. Fluorescent lights, rubbing alcohol, antibacterial hand wash, and electronic beeps and blips flooded our senses for eleven days. Eleven days of a different world, of noise and confusion, of fear and torment.

After those eleven days, Daisy was discharged from the hospital, and we wearily trudged up our front walkway, climbed our three steps, and stood in front of our familiar, old paned-glass front door. While fishing for the keys I looked down and saw a little brown box. Sephora. Instantly I was caught in a crossfire of disgust and rage, of sorrow and regret. How could I have been so stupid? How could I have been that oblivious? I loathed myself; I loathed the box. I loathed that I had spent so much time on something so insignificant, something more a distraction than necessity, and, mostly, I loathed that often the way life goes isn't up to me. That small brown cardboard carton of beauty goals seemed to laugh at me, mock my naiveté. *How could you have wasted a whole hour on this? You think life will go the way you want all the time? Ha!*

My foot shot out and sent that box flying.

Real life showed up without my permission and announced that there would be a change of plans. *We interrupt this regularly scheduled program to inform you that life is precarious and loving people holds no guarantees.* I think up until then I had taken for granted what I had— not grossly, not to the point of completely trampling on all the good stuff, but in a silent, sly, comfortable way. Daisy's diagnosis was a major wake-up call.

The Sephora box settled in the corner, dented ever so slightly. Almost as if it was saying, *Stupid, shallow girl. Your life is out of control. Daisy has cancer, and you just sat like a lump picking out makeup. It probably won't even look good on you.* I hated it. I hated that I hadn't known the state of my own daughter's health. I hated that one minute my life was a breeze, gentle and cool, and then the next it was stifling and all the windows were stuck. I hated that I was without a choice in the matter, that there was no way out of the mess but through it.

Life had pulled a fast one on me, and I felt like I was blindfolded and swinging at a piñata that was way too high. I swung wildly and missed, all while the crowd of onlookers watched my misfortune. I felt embarrassed for spending so much time on that one purchase, for think-ing I had it all under control, for lacking the reason and wisdom a proper mother should have. I had been liv-ing with a set of expectations that I wasn't even aware of. I had expected things to always stay the same. I had expected to not feel great pain in life, to never suffer. I had expected ease. But now I had tasted the shocking flavor of reality. I didn't want any part of it.

As the days after we got home from the hospital melted into each other, something dawned on me. I could sit paralyzed, dumbfounded by our situation, poised to throw in the towel, or I could rise up and participate right where I was. I had a choice. I can't control noninfectious diseases, natural disasters, or heartbreak. I can't control most of the things moms worry about, in fact. But I can control how I spend my time, what's worth my focus and attention, what words I say, how well I love. What was up to me were the small choices, my mindset in this earthly life, and how best to spend my first and only tour on this planet.

When you're flung into a new stage of life, the challenge of keeping up, of learning new habits of being, happens moment by moment. Each moment we are faced with a decision: Will we lean in and invest or let it pass by and miss pivotal and essential parts? One of Daisy's nurses told me about a mother of a newly diagnosed cancer kid who wouldn't stop playing a video game on her phone while the nurse was trying to give her a rundown on how to care for her sick child. Both the nurse and I were appalled at this behavior, yet I've found this same tendency to avoid life in myself. For me, it manifests in other ways—denial, pasting a smile on my face, avoiding relational conflict, or even compulsory shopping and eating—I just happen to not enjoy video games. Also, I'm much better at keeping my dysfunctional tendencies under wraps.

Leaning into real life is super hard. It not only calls for examination, confrontation, and investment, but it takes major courage and continuous practice. I'm still finding this out, even years after my Sephora box episode. As each new season begins, I must intentionally look deep inside with brutal honesty at my expectations and lay them bare before God, willingly trading them for what he has for me and being content in that. Each phase that crops up in life—whether it's raising a teenager, having another baby, starting a new career, or planting another church—calls for courage, because, whether we asked for it or not, it is ripe ground for building a beautiful life or for tearing it down. Everything we walk through cries out to us not to miss it, not to manipulate it to go our way but to just be present in the middle of it. To accept it for what it is, to engage fully and not give away what God has for us during that time in exchange for lesser things.

That's what I call practicing presence. The moment-by-moment, season-by-season continuous investment in what's here and now, not what we wished for. That means our current circumstances, whether it's a cancer diagnosis or nursing twins or studying law at Harvard. It means our actual people, whether sticky toddlers, handsome suitors, or annoying roommates. It means our real unretouched life, whether it's job hunting, raising kids, or rescuing women from modern-day slavery.

I think, at one time, we all had a script we wrote for our lives. One that looked vastly different than what we see here and now. It was a script that refused to be followed, though sometimes it sure looks like the next girl got what she wanted. I'm pretty sure it's not just me, but don't we have this reactive way of looking around and wishing for someone else's talents, someone else's people, someone else's life? We are seldom content with our own. Discontentment seems to be the place we find ourselves most comfortable, and we see fit to set down its insatiable roots.

But regardless of how the script plays out, this is what I've learned: practicing presence nurtures peace and contentment. It does. It's only when we practice presence that we slow down enough to see how lovely our own lives are; it's when we notice all the ways God's hand is on it. It's when we stop and look our people in the face and notice the flecks of gold in our child's eyes, the calluses on our man's hands. It's when we turn down the noise so we can hear the whispers of God's pleasure as we walk with him in our work, when we reflect his glory in our play. It's when we kneel down and inhale the fragrance of Jesus' feet, the ones washed with expensive perfume poured from alabaster by a woman just like you and me, one with a regular life marked by ups and downs. It's when we push the reset button and enter into Sabbath rest. These real-life moments are beautiful, I think, even when we don't stop to recognize it.

❋

There's a funny little book in the Old Testament, one which confronts the ideas of dissatisfaction and discontentment, one that urges us to practice presence. Ecclesiastes has always been a strange part of the Bible to me. And, thanks to The Byrds, I get a curious compulsion to make a flower crown and slip on my Birkenstocks every time I read it. But aside from my own cultural rendition of this ancient book of wisdom, it has come to have new meaning for me.

We know the "time for" verses. We can sing them in our heads, but if we back up and read the beginning of the book, it's kind of a downer. You see, with all the talk of "everything is completely meaningless," Ecclesiastes has become one of those biblical books we wave off nonchalantly or sweep under the rug. The one that asks more questions than it answers, which is in total opposition to the neat and tidy Christianity so many of us grew up with. And it's especially puzzling following the book of Proverbs, which heartily assures us that if we just work hard, stay away from cute boys, and choose the way of wisdom, we will be okay—we'll glide breezily through life, even. *If you just do A, B, and C, you'll surely be blessed!* Easy peasy.

Ah, if only.

Ecclesiastes shows us the other side of the coin. The book goes something like this: The Teacher in Ecclesiastes is trying to understand the meaning of life. He finds it to be elusive and, at first glance, somewhat depressing. The phrase "everything is completely meaningless" is used over and over. Different translations use different words in this phrase: *meaningless, vanity, futility,* or *pointless.* In Hebrew, the word is *hevel,* which translates as "vapor" or "smoke." He is saying life is temporary, impossible to grab onto or control, unpredictable. He describes the way life goes, how we invest time and energy into great things like work, wisdom, or pleasure, and yet we can't control the outcome. He admits that there is no guarantee of the wise prospering or the wicked getting their due justice. He declares everything in life to be vapor, or meaningless, and so he questions how we should live in light of it all. Do we seek pleasure? Wealth? Wisdom? Hedonism? If we can't control anything, then why bother?

I have been in that place, feeling a bit like life is meaningless, cruel even. I can't control the outcome. I can't make my life match my personal fairy-tale script. So much of the time, we wish we could trade in our circumstances, prove the Teacher wrong, show him that life is not meaningless, not *hevel.* But slowly we come to understand what the Teacher is saying and face the reality of the fact that we are all going to die, some of us sooner than others, but perhaps there is still something of worth there, something we can't see. Something that could give us a little hint as to how to live well, not just survive.

And right in that vein of thinking, there's a verse from this short introspective book that calls out to me.

Right there, tucked in after the dance of the seasons, after the summation of the human life experience on earth, there is a chorus that is perfectly timed. It sings out softly to me from the din of life and death and everything in between, asking if I will listen.

The Teacher questions the reader in chapter 3, verses 9 through 11, "What do people really get for all their hard work? I have seen the burden God has placed on us all. *Yet God has made everything beautiful for its own time.* He has planted eternity in the human heart, but even so, people cannot see the whole scope of God's work from beginning to end" (emphasis mine).

God has made everything beautiful *for its own time.* But don't we want to just get through it some or most of the time? Don't we want to shut out the times that aren't particularly lovely? Or sometimes the loveliness is too great and we shield our eyes. But we are told there is purpose and beauty in each season, in each circumstance. That eternity is in our hearts, but we are only able to see what's right in front of us, *and that's okay.* This makes us uncomfortable because it calls us to be openhanded with everything we've got: the number of our days, our life's work, our play, even our communion with God and man. We are not meant to see it all at once. We are meant to breathe in today, and only today.

God is calling us to be active participants in our own lives, and collectively we are finding it to be a challenge. The way of satisfaction and contentment is out there.

The way of faith and courage is laid before us. I didn't see them so blatantly before, but now I realize God has been offering me these nuggets of fresh air my whole life—it was just up to me to stop and notice. That Sephora box kicked off some pivotal years for me, where I had no choice but to hear what God was saying in the fray.

I don't have the secret to life; I don't have the formula for monastic contentment or the impressive ability to be present. But I do know it's something in the quieting of the soul. The resting of the eyes, the still place where we stop and listen. When the Spirit of God is allowed a voice. When we are brave enough to listen to what he has to say. It's in the deep places, the ones that take us to maturity. It's in the courage to listen, yes, but also the courage to obey. To be fruitful right now, exactly where we are. And it's dang hard. But it's good and it's real.

This is a journey that, for me, began many years ago and continues still. It involves faith, love, hope. It includes travel, food, naked people, courage, real life, holidays, new friends, and new traditions. It's about work and play, community, daily rhythms; it's about the moments that make up a life. It's a journey to presence. To going off the grid and living life with intentionality. To choosing peace over chaos, little by little turning down the noise, one discovery at a time. It's a journey to quickening the desperation for contentment and inviting the good, true, and beautiful. Let's walk in this together. Lay down the chaos and be prepared to get your breath back.

two

BAGGAGE CLAIM

S o, do you think I should get a vasectomy?" Britt said while passing me in the hallway one bright summer afternoon.

Daisy had just turned one year old, and our son was four. We had the perfectly proportioned family for our conventional white-picket-fence existence, and it was time to start thinking of our reproductive future. Or lack of it. All our friends were going the snip-snip route, so naturally we considered it for ourselves. The copycat mentality is alive and well way past middle school, and because women are grossly and inappropriately informed on the details of all our besties' reproductive health and choices, a vasectomy was next on our to-do list.

I remember stopping a moment in the sunshine that was pouring through the hall window, flagstone patio and olive trees in my peripheral vision, laundry basket balanced on my hip. Casually I responded, "Um, nah. I mean, what if one of our kids dies? I wouldn't want to be a one-kid family."

He looked at me as if we were deciding whether to get tacos or burritos for lunch, shrugged, and said, "Okay."

Okay, as if we had just decided what color to paint

the bathroom. *Okay,* as if we were simply considering putting bunk beds in our son's bedroom.

Fast-forward seven years, and Daisy was, in fact, dying. And I was, in fact, about to be the mother of a one-kid family. Daisy was losing her fight with cancer, and we were out of treatment options, having exhausted all the approved regimens American pediatric oncology offered. After getting her third diagnosis—the one that came with the dreaded "we've done all we can do" death sentence—our attention, time, and efforts were caught in a deluge. The mission to find an alternative cure took over. We sent out mass pleas for help on social media and received an avalanche of replies, everything from "eat copious amounts of this certain nut" and "drink mushroom tea" to "have this extra-holy person pray for her." We had to weed through the noise and the crazy, all while bearing the leaden weight of holding Daisy's life in our hands.

It was up to me and her dad to make the critical choice of what we should do, and it felt like a sick game of Russian roulette. After the rigidity of traditional cancer treatment, choosing an alternative and experimental treatment was like standing before some cruel and brazen carnival lady in garish lipstick spinning the wheel. If we picked the right number we would win it all, but if not . . . There seemed to be a hundred ways to treat Daisy and a hundred ways to die. All we had to do was clearly hear from the Lord about which choice was the winning number; then we'd know which direction to take our family, our future. *No pressure.* My world was a whirlwind of chaos, a frantic effort to hear the voice of God, to do right by my family. After much agonizing, much prayer, and with the generous financial help of many, we decided on a clinic in Israel where a brilliant doctor was developing innovative ways to treat cancer.

Even after we made the decision, though, my brain swarmed with medical conversations, outreach on social media, wacky suggestions, visas, correspondence with the Israeli clinic, treatment trials, and all the medical preparations to get us there. It felt like the four of us were about to jump off a bridge, holding hands and hoping we wouldn't get separated. When the time finally came and all our emergency visas were granted, we packed our sandals and to the Holy Land we went.

I was about to learn some of the most valuable lessons of my life, things I couldn't have imagined ever needing to learn. There are some lessons that, when they transpire, it's like finally noticing your roots are badly outgrown or the jeans you've been wearing twice a week make your butt look lumpy. *How have I been walking around like this? Why did I think it was completely okay?*

Funny how God works, keeping quiet about stuff until it's time. It's like he keeps us on a "need to know" basis, when sometimes we would appreciate a little heads-up. Or perhaps even a spreadsheet with dates, times, lists, and little boxes we can check off with a satisfactory grunt. But more often the lessons come with flesh, with breath, with dust and sweat and holy moments. For us, they came covered in rocks and dirt, in hipster Tel Aviv cafes. They came in Orthodox Jewish families, in the lighting of the Shabbat candles. They came on bloody knees, in hotel buffets, in the brown faces and bright smiles of Mediterranean surfers, and in sound waves through the car stereo. The lessons came in dry cracked earth, and they came in torrential downpours.

Thank God, they came.

＊

We arrived in Israel with some baggage. There were suitcases full of surf tee shirts, modest long skirts, favorite stuffed animals, math books, and Bibles. We packed surfboards and shampoo and swimsuits. There were bulging bags with all of our needs and some of our wants; after all, we weren't sure if we were going to be there three months or twelve. But then there was our *baggage*. The baggage packed inside our hearts from three years of cancer treatment, from cure research and blogs. From raising kids and raising a church, from friendships and broken hearts. And from all the voices and choices, the fast-paced, noisy, busy life we were living.

When we arrived at our first landing place, a hotel in Tel Aviv, our bags took up the entire room. I honestly don't know how we fit it all in our teeny little rental car, which looked like a Happy Meal toy with the surfboards strapped to the roof and my six-foot-six-inch husband behind the wheel, knees bent up by his ears. We had tried to save money and had booked a small room, but, as we wearily dropped our monstrous bags on the floor, we realized there would be no space to move. Or breathe. The baggage had gotten the best of us all.

While I sat on the bed and tried not to cry in front of the kids, Britt headed straight to the front desk to plead our case. And so, we waited, sitting on the polyester bedspreads in that cramped room on the thirteenth floor, staring at each other, eyes round with apprehension as we sighed over the mounds of stuff that stood between us. Isn't that so often the way our baggage is? Piled up between us and those closest to us. We don't see it until we are in a situation where its magnitude can't be ignored, when you can't even move because of its sheer weight. Slowing down and even stopping is the surest way to discover what kind of baggage we carry around, particularly the kind of baggage that's been drowning out the goodness of life, the kind that perpetuates our discontentment. And there's nothing like slowing down to a complete stop in a foreign country—free from all our familiar distractions, all our familiar sounds—to make us face our junk.

All was silent at the beginning of our journey, and the silence was nearly deafening after a long and loud season. It was a new beginning of sorts, a chance to snap out of it so that we could dive into it. And in that silence, the true sounds and textures and melodies of life were given a place to begin to break through. When we quiet ourselves and our thoughts are allowed out of their cages, it can be a scary thing. But a beautiful one. My baggage was due for inspection, and it was time to lay it all out, time to face what was taking up so much heart space and leaving no room for flourishing in our circumstances.

It was in the involuntary slowing down that I began to see how my baggage had gotten the best of me. I could see that I was trying to race through the hard parts of life, my awful circumstances. I had been trying to make sense of it by searching for a cure, by reaching out to anyone and everyone, by keeping a smile on my face for my kids and not allowing myself to really enter into the feelings without some type of guard up. And it was the silence we found ourselves in that showed me these things. Stopping and opening up the suitcase to see what I had unknowingly packed for my life journey. Some of it was needed, yes. Things like questions and doubts are always acceptable and can lead us to good places if we let them. But others simply took up space between me and my people, me and God: overconnection, busyness, stress, noise, desensitization, pain avoidance.

My first instinct when it's time to be still is to evade the tough stuff, because that's when the unprocessed pain comes up or when I learn something new about myself. It's in the quiet moments when I unearth my real life, when the parts I've tried to shove down are allowed a bit of daylight. That can be scary, I know. But that's also when the good comes. That's when the secret love letters are whispered, when the mysterious beauty of creation, family, of a deep breath and a beautiful meal is truly experienced. That's when the work really gets done, like sitting down to flesh out what God is saying in the stillness to me, to you.

Getting outside ourselves is often an exercise in getting in. Into our brains, into our souls. Into our messy hearts that scare the crud out of us. Quieting down forces us to face our stuff. I'm guessing it's different for each of us depending on our life's experiences, relational tendencies, or where we're at with God. For me and my family, it showed us that endless summer is a myth. We can chase it all we want, but it's not ours to grasp.

It was definitely not in my script to move my family to Israel so that we could get our daughter last-ditch-effort cancer treatment. If it were up to me, I would have all my ducks in a row, wouldn't embrace risk, wouldn't have any reason to feel too deeply. I would keep life on the surface, keep pain and disruption at bay. I would stay in that middle space of safety, of ease. But to be honest, though that is my inclination, I would probably dry up and blow away. Surface living sounds fun for a bit, but ultimately it isn't sustainable.

Going to Israel was a gift. It was frightening and stressful and difficult at times, but it was saturated with opportunity. Change is like that. We hate when we don't know what's coming; we hate that we can't control our outcomes. We want all of life to stay the same: comfortable, routine. But, listen, when change comes, we must walk right into it. When we drop our bags and see what's coming between us and real life, we must be willing to flow and move and grow, to face our fears, to pluck out the pleasures.

We must walk right into it, yes, but we start where we can. I'm talking baby steps, small beginnings. And since we laid our baggage down right where we were, right in our own context, our own space, we did what we knew to do. We started with breakfast. Allow me to explain.

Over the course of my relationship with Britt, food has always been a major player in our game. Beginning when we first started dating, Britt and I have always made regular visits to the hole-in-the-wall Mexican joints in our little town. We could do a blindfolded taste test and tell you which burrito we're eating and where it's from. This one? Oh, easy, that's carnitas from Michael's Beach Liquor. Reynaldo's breakfast burrito! Chile relleno from Reyes', for sure. California burrito from Taco Grande, hands down. Rudy's bean, rice, and cheese! You name it, we ate it. But not only did we eat burritos profusely, we fought over them like a couple of stray dogs. There is a fifteen-inch height difference between us, and since my man is able to make a burrito disappear in a blink, I've always had to guard mine with my life.

So, when we packed up our lives to go to Israel, trying our darndest to make the best of a horrifying situation, we found something to look forward to together, and that something was food.

Food is such an integral part of humanity. We have to eat, but we don't always receive it for the gift it is. Rather than gathering around tables as families, lovers, and communities, we inhale something wrapped in paper on our laps while driving across town with a carload of salty young surfers or top-knotted ballerinas. Rather than stopping to give thanks, to receive the blessing of nourishment and flavor and togetherness, we suck down something through a straw or we drown out our experience with noise obscuring the conversation. Food has become merely mechanical, not medicinal, and our approach to it has tended toward selfishness rather than thoughtfulness.

I love the thought of mealtimes in ancient civilization, specifically in Bible times, and being that we were in the Holy Land, it was the central context for our experience. The idea of John leaning into Jesus, the way they savored their simple meals, the pouring of the wine and the blessing of the family. The image of Jesus looking up at his Father while breaking bread. Herbs and oils, aromatic and ample. I imagine the candlelight flickering on Peter's bearded face, eyes twinkling as he debated with James about which of them had cast out more demons. I picture Mary Magdalene hanging on to Jesus' every

word, bursting out loudly in laughter over his jokes, spilling a bit of lentil soup on her tunic. And I'm smelling the
pots of stew, the fresh yeasty scent of pita cooked on a
hot stone, the saucers of hummus slowly disappearing as
hands tearing the bread brush each other across the table
while dipping.

Mealtimes are a gift. They are a time to stop what we
are doing, whether work or play, and refill the body. And
because we are whole beings, the mind and spirit become
recharged as well. How have we forgotten the beautiful
significance of this very primal activity, this ancient
vehicle of connectivity and sustenance? What have we
become that we throw this gift away? Is it really worth
it to disregard the majority of our mealtimes and merely
shove food in our faces while we tend to more important things like getting back to work? Or getting to the
next event? Britt and I decided that there's no time like
the present, and getting back to mealtime magic sounded
like a balm to our souls.

Enter the breakfast buffet. Israeli buffets are beyond
awesome. Not only are they teeming with color and flavor, but they are full of exotic items Americans don't
really consider "breakfast." Fish, for example. Whole
fish with scales and eyeballs. And vegetables. Piles of
the bright green cucumbers and vibrant red tomatoes
of the quintessential Israeli salad. And, girl, the cheese.
Soft cheese, hard cheese, cheese with names I can't pro-
nounce. Smooth mounds of cheese for smearing on toast,

uniform rows of triangular and rectangular slices, ombré in shades of yellows and creams and whites. There are stacks of breads of every kind: sweet rolls, rolls to be stuffed with butter, and sliced bread for toasting, grainy and nutty and brown. There are olives galore, slick with oil and covered in fresh herbs. There are shiny trays filled with slippery white hard-boiled eggs, and, if it is a particularly traditional buffet, there is shakshuka. Shakshuka is a dish made with tomatoes, onions, and peppers, swimming in garlic and spices with an egg cooked in the middle—yolk slightly runny. Oh, man.

So, the two of us—used to inhaling food our entire lives, whether it was out of the probability the other would steal the best bite, or out of necessity while balancing a cafeteria platter on our laps in a hospital room, or because we wolfed it down in the hallway out of respect for Daisy who often wasn't able to eat—decided it was time to slow it down. To connect, to notice each other and our surroundings, to tune in to the gift of food, the luxury of time, and the precious people in front of us.

I remember that first Israeli breakfast. In an attempt to bring a fun vibe to a desperate situation, Britt had on a button-down we dubbed his "party shirt" with a straw fedora tipped at a jaunty angle atop his whiskery head he had shaved in solidarity with Daisy. I decided to wear a dress with pretty sandals (gladiators—sorry, ancient occupied Israel, but they're my favorite style), and we felt fancy. After the initial cooing over the food and carping at Isaiah to put something other than pure sugar on his plate, we settled into our seats. We bowed our heads, said thanks to God, and after taking a deep breath, we sank into the first bite.

Enjoying breakfast became a thing for us, a new habit of being. We set our forks down between bites, talked excitedly of what else we would try, analytically took in the other diners we shared the high-rise dining room with. We gazed out on the urban sprawl of Tel Aviv, the young city a grid of muted tans and geometric shapes, dotted with white by the solar water heaters that covered each building. We brought a deck of pink playing cards and took our time at the table. We had unspoken wars with another visiting family over who got to the dining room first and claimed the best table. We marveled over the massive stack of bread a table of three little old babushka ladies packed away every day. We convinced ourselves that the immaculately dressed blond couple we saw daily were Russian spies. We enjoyed the drift of words we didn't understand, spoken in an ancient language all around us—a new and unfamiliar yet beguiling song. We savored each other's faces, savored the food, and gave sincere thanks.

Baggage inspection showed us that it was time to slow down, take a deep breath, and enter into our season with intentionality. And breakfast became the first habit that kept us in that place; it gave us the chance to begin our day with introspection, with gratitude. Breakfast was centering: instead of barreling into the mess and stress of our days, it gave us space to stop, breathe in what was most important that day, and breathe out what God didn't mean for us to carry.

We started small, smack in the middle of awful. By God's grace and his loving baggage inspection, we grabbed hold of what we could. Change came and it came swiftly, but we opened our eyes and searched for the fullness; we opened our arms and welcomed what God had for us. Right in the buffet line, plunged in hard times.

We underwent a bit of open-heart surgery during those days. There were things we had to let go of. First of all, control. We had to learn to give God what was his in the first place. We had to figure out how to hand over our longing for different circumstances, to accept what was our reality. We prayed and wrestled and grappled. We read and sought and scrutinized. And, by God's grace, we were up for the challenge to enter into contentment, to choose to see what was good. Not in the past, not in the hoped-for future. Not in someone else's life, but in our own currently adverse lives.

Being in Israel taught me much, and as I reminisce and go back and ask questions of myself and God, I hope you'll join me in your own holy pilgrimage. Drop your baggage with me; be willing to open it up, lay the contents out on the bed, and see what's in there. See what's beautiful on you and what is ill fitting. See what will come in handy later and what you need right now.

Be prepared to give a place to the real life calling out to you instead of stuffing it in the dresser to be forgotten. Get ready to take that first small step. Let's trust God together with what he will do in the quiet spaces and in the times of change. Let's trust him to replace some chaos for peace, to bring relief where our lungs are searing, to unearth treasures of what's here today, and to release the surplus.

Because, listen, as I write this, I think, *I've got this! I'm the perspective lady. I'm the presence queen!* But I'm hearing whispers that there is more for me, that even after our Holy Land pilgrimage and all the life I've lived, the death I've witnessed, there are still further places I haven't gone with God that he wants to take me. And isn't it just when we think we've got a hold on something that we learn we were mistaken? That we might be off to a good start, but in reality, we have just barely scratched the surface? That's me. And it might be you too.

It's time to revisit lessons I've learned, time to take them further. It's time to inspect my baggage again, to see what has snuck in there since the last time I cleaned it out. It's time to ask the harder questions, to cultivate deeper contentment. It's time to confront what I'm afraid of, what I feel I'm entitled to, and that comparison that plays nasty tricks on me. I'm prepared to be unpleasantly surprised, to unearth stuff that I thought only existed in other people. I'm prepared to find something sparkly in myself and in the offerings of a God who loves me. I'm prepared to do hard work, to reflect, rethink, repent, and rejoice. And I'm prepared to laugh at myself and other people, because, after all, the human species is comedy at its best.

three

#KILLYOURWIFI

When we were preparing our family and our hearts for Israel, in the stifling sterility of the hospital stays and the never-ending waits of the clinic appointments, we mulled over what we wanted our lives to look like in the upcoming season and what it would take to achieve that. Daily treatments and drives into Tel Aviv were in store, but we would have weekends free and all the Jewish holidays. Our priorities had become stick straight, and one thing was patently clear: we refused to trade what was right here and right now for what was elsewhere. We knew this trip would be full of hard things, but we also saw our opportunity to scoop up as much as possible—of each other, of God, of wild and tangible life. Not wanting to miss a single moment, we made a decision that would not only help us make the most of that opportunity but would also change the trajectory of our lives after Israel in a huge way.

Cannonballing directly into the deep end, we went off the grid. We limited our computer usage to weekly emails with family and occasional updates on Daisy's blog. We left our iPhones behind and rented simple flip phones that only worked in Israel. We went off our social media. We arranged it so that there was no way to immediately get ahold of us: no notifications, no texts, no calls, no noise. It was a fresh start, an exhilarating experiment in observation, participation, and intimate communication. It was a complete abandonment of the familiar—the illusory sense of connection to the world—and it was like finally getting that rock out of my boot that was constantly vying for my attention. We were flying free, no strings, no distractions. Just us.

Our choice to go off the grid in Israel may be extreme to some, but for us, it seemed like a natural progression. My family has a bit of a reputation for being a little . . . old-fashioned. Some might even call us hillbillies. Mostly this is technologically speaking, although the camouflage freezer filled with venison in our hay shed suggests we lean toward the wild and free. We've never had cable television, don't have internet, and I'm the only person in the family with an iPhone. I'd like to say we also play the banjo and square-dance in the evenings, but that's just not true. Oh, and either gag or cheer, but we own all of *Little House on the Prairie* on DVD. That sounded like a confession you hear in one of those industrial-carpeted rooms surrounded by fidgety people in metal folding chairs. *My name is Kate, and I'm a huge fan of Michael Landon.* There, I said it. I feel better now.

Listen, each of us has only twenty-four hours in a day, and our days are numbered. All day every day we are faced with choices. We only have so much time and attention we can give, and we only have so much capacity for communication, information, news, or enter-tainment. We should be picky, don't you think? I like to think of all our daily intake choices—what we read, what we watch, what we listen to, who we spend time with—in terms of diet. That's probably because I'm from California, and I'm pretty sure it's a state requirement to be gluten intolerant as well as be able to recognize three different types of kale. And, as my friend Sarah recently reminded me, I've been on plenty of diets in the last twenty years. We're talking the Cabbage Soup Diet, Atkins, UltraMetabolism, Paleo, Keto, and most recently, the mother of all diets, Whole30.

Whole30 is like boot camp for health. It's glorious and gut-wrenching; it's maddening and empowering. Basically, Whole30 is an elimination diet aiming to pinpoint all the things we generally get addicted to but are hurting us at a cellular level, sometimes showing up more obviously in the form of joint pain, weight gain, or skin conditions. For thirty days, you must cut out all grains, sugars, alcohol (even vanilla extract!), dairy, and legumes. All the foods our bodies can tend to have issues with, which is pretty much everything I want to eat. When the thirty days are up, you reintroduce the elimi-nated foods, one at a time, so you know the effect these foods have on you. It's hard, man.

While I started off like a boss, the enticement of gluten, dairy, and sugar was too powerful to be ignored. And going the way of all my previous diets, I crashed and burned like a drone on Christmas morning. In fact, once, when at a dinner party and meeting a popular blogger and cookbook author, I tried to be cool and relate with her by saying I used to be Paleo. She asked me why I wasn't anymore, and I could only mutter "pizza." Then I turned away for the walk of shame.

Sugar is even worse for me than cheese. Since I have a voracious sweet tooth, I know that if I have sugar in my house I will eat it. All of it. Over the trash can so the kids don't notice. I'm not even kidding. Case in point: just recently I made my youngest, Fifi, chocolate cupcakes for her birthday. From scratch, with huge mounds of home-made buttercream adorning the top like a Russian palace, pink with pastel sprinkles. Pleasantly surprised that the recipe yielded twenty-four rather than the twelve I had planned on, I thought I'd do the world a favor and eat three of them that day. One straight from the pan, and two at the party. No problem. It doesn't count when you eat standing up, or something like that. Until the next day. I brought Fifi home from church and, without stopping, headed straight to the plate of leftover cup-cakes. With my back turned, hunched over the trash can, I inhaled two more before Fifi had the chance to notice. I don't even know what happened—my old habits sidled back up and took me down, the wrappers snickering at the frosting on my lip. But no one ate those cupcakes for me; I just got sucked along with the temptation tide.

Episodes like this remind me that I need to generally

keep unhealthy food out of the house, knowing that if it's there it will end up in my belly. So why don't we do this with all the other things we consume? Why do we allow all the stuff that is junky for us at the soul level to creep in and affect our emotional and spiritual wellness? Just like our physical health, what's inside eventually manifests outwardly, and if we crowd it with the wrong things, what eventually comes out is jealousy, discontentment, self-loathing, and dissatisfaction. So how should we approach the spiritual equivalent to Whole30? Basically, if something doesn't make us healthier, then we shouldn't consume much of it. And sometimes, if the effect is detrimental, we need to do without it altogether. We do well to choose judiciously, to put one thing down so that we can pick the better thing up.

Just like I know I need help putting the cupcake down so I can pick up something healthier, I've learned to put tech down for the same reason. If I have wifi at home, I know I will get lost in a wormhole of blogs and videos and distraction. Britt's the same way. We opted for a limited data plan on my phone so I can't zone out endlessly on a screen, but it still lets me do what I need to do online. And for entertainment, we have the actual DVD subscription to Netflix. Yes, that's still a thing. It's like being on a media diet, not because I'm so holy, but because I'm not.

Since our days are numbered I decided I'd rather not spend too much of it online. There are already enough secondary matters vying for my attention. Isn't it strange how quickly life piles up? If we don't take care of our mail, it can spill out the door and carry us with it, a paper tidal wave of catalogs and solicitations and bills. Or we get bogged down and held hostage by all the little things that worm their way into our lives—emails, texts, this Voxer message, that Evite. And let's not forget about the head-lines and voices shouting from every corner of the internet about current events and what you should think about them. We end up living in a state of defeat or numbness or both. Some of these obligations are pressed upon us, but others we take on ourselves because we believe culture is telling us we have to live this way. We wonder how on earth our brain space got cluttered up to the point of a robotic and forced existence. We wonder why we end up on autopilot, unfeeling and dead inside.

It happens to everyone, this overcrowded life. Like a pushy salesman, it just wedges its foot in the door, won't take no for an answer, and spreads its extraneous wares before us until we relent and buy it all. We have failed to unsubscribe, to say, "No, thank you," to think for ourselves. We buy whatever is solicited; we rhyth-mically nod in a stupor to all the voices that say they will make our lives better with whatever drivel they're selling. From online chatter to information and enter-tainment overconsumption, we exist in a constant state of overwhelm. The siren call of excess lures us in, prom-ises to fulfill, and, like drunken sailors, we go overboard until we're sunk. Somehow, we say yes to these things without thinking them through first, without counting the cost—that every single thing we bring into our minds and homes and lives costs time and attention that has to come from somewhere—usually from the things and people most important to us.

That's no way to live. Has no one told us that just because something's offered, it doesn't mean we should accept? That everything has a cost that we might not be willing to pay? That just because the whole group is going along with it doesn't mean we have to? But that's where it starts, isn't it? Asking ourselves these questions. Asking what direction our current choices are leading us. It takes awareness, seeing what we've filled ourselves with, and the audacity to do without.

❖

Have you ever taken medication for a problem as benign as acne but realized the solution came with the threat of depression, suicidal thoughts, heart palpitations, and so on? Sometimes the side effects of what's meant to help are worse than the actual disease. When my family and I went off the grid, it was like we woke up. We became aware of the side effects some of our past tech choices had caused in our lives. We hadn't even realized we were suffocating under a pile of communication before— between the traffic on Daisy's blog, the endless emails, texts, Britt's Twitter, and my Instagram. Being so easily available to anyone and everyone had resulted in the high cost of time away from our kids, emotional investment in drama that wasn't our business, and the thinning of patience as we gave of ourselves to too many. We figured out that inboxes never resolve themselves; they only result in more work, more time spent staring at a screen. And the connectivity that promised community only resulted in loneliness and burnout.

Finally away from constant distraction for the first time since the invention of the cell phone, we saw it all for what it was—and it was crying out to be put in its place. And surprise! No one died when we reprioritized our use of technology. In fact, the noisy, sticky, insatiable monster shrank back when we didn't constantly feed it. Miraculously, the burdensome pile dissipated when we didn't hover over it, constantly fretting. Stuff still got done, and nothing imploded because we weren't constantly available. Our use of tech and connection and availability all just needed to be put into submission.

Maybe that was what we'd been missing before: the permission to draw lines, boundaries that aren't necessarily for keeping others out but for keeping ourselves intact. If loving others is the second most important commandment and we couldn't make it happen with those closest to us because we were too busy with everyone and everything else, then it was time to make a change before we found ourselves in a desperate situation.

Eyes wide open and distraction-free, my family and I forged our way through the terrifying and blessed life we found ourselves in the middle of that fall in Israel. It's amazing what you see, feel, and hear when you're fully present. No iPhone meant no outside influence. It meant no interruptions, no persuasion other than what was in front of our faces; it meant we spent our days together sharing the same real-life experiences, not the ones fabricated on a screen.

The days were so real, so full of breath and sound and taste. The long drives we took, singing along to Matisyahu's *Spark Seeker* at the top of our lungs. The walks through the cobbled streets of Jaffa while we counted stray cats. The hummus and pita at Abu Hassan shared with new and old friends. The sun on our backs while hiking through the countryside. The night sky punctuated by lightning while dining outdoors at the nature reserve in the Carmel Valley. The families we watched while enjoying gelato on the grass at the ancient ruins of Caesarea. The smell of shawarma, tangy and mouthwatering. All for us, all so good.

I look back on those days, on what we could have easily missed, and I remember how good it was, even in a weird and sad time. It reminds me of how strongly I feel about keeping overconnection and distraction in its place, and when it starts to sneak in again—the temptation of overdoing the use of technology or the lure of habitually looking at my phone—I remember that too many cupcakes make me sick. That glutting on connection is like hunching over the trash can, consuming something that eventually has a cost. It's never worth it.

※

Setting down one thing for another sets us up for celebration, but it's not the easiest thing to do, not generally our first inclination. In fact, we need help getting there. We need someone to tell us when to stop, to give us permission to set our distractions and work and striving aside and just be.

That permission came for us when Britt and I read a book called *Living into Focus*. It introduced us to the concept of focal activities, which ended up being a reminder of the things we truly loved in life. Things we tended to lose sight of in the clamor and fast pace of daily living. Focal activities are things that are done without immediate gratification, things that take time, effort, and singular focus. But they're things with an eventual payoff, things that delight the senses in the process.

Cooking is a primary one. It's done slowly and requires concentration and total presence, but you get to experience the aromas and textures and flavors. Walking is another example, as it's not something to be rushed and allows time for praying, thinking, worship, or listening to something smart or funny or interesting. Then there's gardening, which is a slow process and requires patience and effort yet yields something to show for it. The idea is, life is better, more meaningful, when we engage in activities that have true and hard-earned benefits. It's a practice of *real*.

In our current tech-obsessed fast-paced culture, engaging in anything slow or challenging almost calls for a complete reprogramming of the mind. We are told that doing things for ourselves rather than letting a machine do it for us is outdated and exhausting. We are sold a lifestyle of fast food, the easy way, and the lie that unless it's behind a screen it's too much work. I wonder what on earth has possessed us to think that lying on the couch glued to a phone or computer is a better and more blessed activity than cooking for someone you love, or that constantly zoning out on mindless entertainment is more blessed than being creative with our own minds and hands. It's almost like we've given a piece of our hearts and souls away in the name of efficiency and productivity. And yet it seems like we're more vexed than ever, living in a world dominated by what others say and think. But we continue on in our fast-paced ways.

I see how we take the soul of real life and trade it for the strange addiction to control and hustle. What is it about the hustle? Is it the affirmation we are looking for? Maybe for some. Or perhaps, if you're like me, you believe that if you stay busy enough or entertained enough or have enough control over a situation it will be a safeguard against pain. Some of us hustle because if we stop, we won't be able to stand the silence—the voices we hear inside our heads have potential to hurt, so we never give them a chance to speak. It's almost like someone else has to stop us from constantly running because we aren't so good at stopping ourselves.

Enter Shabbat. Nowhere on earth is there a more beautiful system in place to stifle the hustle than Israel. Observing Shabbat, or Sabbath, is honoring a commandment made to the Jews to rest every seventh day. And when the Jews rest, they *rest*. They gather with their families and friends, they break the bread during the blessings, they feast and turn their focus from the week of working and striving to a mandated celebration of God's goodness. Candles and prayers, bread and wine, abundance and blessing. Just family, friends, food, and mandatory downtime. Sounds heavenly, right?

The Orthodox Jews like to kick everything up a notch, or rather, thirty-nine notches. That's how many categories of rules the ancient rabbis decided should be kept on Sabbath, but, God help me, some rules are just begging me to break them. So let's keep it simple and go back to the original mandate for rest. In Exodus 20:8–11 we read,

> Remember to observe the Sabbath day by keeping it holy. You have six days each week for your ordinary work, but the seventh day is a Sabbath day of rest dedicated to the LORD your God. On that day no one

in your household may do any work. This includes you, your sons and daughters, your male and female servants, your livestock, and any foreigners living among you. For in six days the LORD made the heavens, the earth, the sea, and everything in them; but on the seventh day he rested. That is why the LORD blessed the Sabbath day and set it apart as holy.

Basically, God is telling us to take a load off once a week, that we need rest, we can't do it all, and there's a light at the end of the tunnel. Get through hump day, and if we can hold out until Friday night, there's a party coming! And in Israel, it was a party indeed. Any given Friday up until 1:00 p.m., you'd find the shops bustling, the challah selling out fast, Jewish women picking up last-minute goodies for the weekly holiday. On the highway (really!) there were flower stands laden with bright bouquets where young men and women could stop on the way to Mama's house to pick up something lovely to offer. And by 3:00, any grocery store, Jewish café, or juice stand was shuttered down tight. In fact, once I needed to buy a loaf of challah at the grocery store, and the security guard wouldn't let me through as it was almost 3:00. Not knowing much Hebrew but understanding the culture a bit, all I said was "challah!" in a panicky voice, and I was granted entrance. I even got the prized loaf for a few shekels off.

Every week we watched families piling into each

other's apartments, smelled the aroma of the feast they would enjoy together. A few times, new friends invited us to take part, and we delightedly took in the holiness of the evening, the words recited from the Scripture, the blessings given sons, daughters, and wife, hands on heads and hearts on sleeves. One Jewish woman who allowed me to join in her preparations asked me to light the Shabbat candles with her, and the magic of the moment rocked me. Together we lit a candle for each child, for each of our husbands, and, finally, we lit a candle for *HaShem* ("the Name" in Hebrew, another way to speak of God). When the candles were lit, my new friend waved her hands over them to usher in God's presence, swooping and fluid, almost like she was wafting the scent of a freshly baked apple pie deep into her lungs. Transfixed, I watched the mother and young daughter share this moment, this celebration of beauty and rest. Tables were set, candles glowed, and by the time the sun disappeared behind the hills, Shabbat had officially begun.

Shabbat lasts not only the entire evening but through the next day until the third star appears in the night sky. All day the people feast, visit, and rest, as the work has already been done. It was so beautiful, so holy. And so fun! The Jews get to do this every week? How have we been pushing ourselves to the limit and ignoring God's commandment to slow down and relax on a regular basis? Who do we think we are that we don't need to heed his Word, that we push and go and never stop, thinking we are indispensable, that maybe God meant that rest is for normal people, but not for us? Why don't we trust God with slowing down? Why don't we trust him with rest?

As we saw this joyful weekly observance and the way it brought families together, the way it brought the hustle to a halt, we decided we wanted in on the action. Our family of four barely had space to sit in our little apartment, so we set the table on the balcony to look out over the outer fringe of Tel Aviv with its parking lots and sandy hills. I picked up the challah from the market down the way, and Isaiah cut up cucumbers and tomatoes and arranged them on a platter surrounding a saucer of hummus. We enjoyed spiced meat, oily olives, and unnamed cheeses. We spread them out on the table, admiring our group effort and the way the colors all set each other off. Straight and proud, we sat under Britt's headship while he recited the blessings over us. We broke the bread; we tasted the wine. We raucously and repeatedly sang out, *Shabbat shalom, hey!* while the evening breeze caressed our faces. Shabbat arrived at the same time each week, and it felt extravagant.

We endeavored to celebrate those Friday nights in Israel, and most of the time we did. We came to look forward to it, to the quiet and lovely end to the week. Shabbat became holy permission: permission to rest, to play, to eat, to sing, to love. It took away the guilt of never stopping and replaced it with the reminder that this was sacred obedience. It gave us a feeling of reward for a week well lived. But the most important thing we learned through celebrating Shabbat was that our lives had become overly stuffed with things we thought we had to do, noise we thought we had to listen to, work that wasn't ours to accomplish. You see, life and all that comes with it is a needy creature. The needs are great, yes, but they aren't all ours to meet. God knows, we need weekly reminders.

✳

Just this week my husband invited a couple of guys over to eat and hang out. We were all standing around the kitchen island polishing off some smoked gouda and bar-becued sausages, while the conversation drifted over to the Ten Commandments. Now, keep in mind, there were three pastors and one pastor's wife. We were trying to name what all ten commandments were, and all four of us were stumped. I got about six of them, and the guys did better with eights and nines. But no one could nail all ten. Adultery, murder, idolatry . . . hmmm . . . what was it? After a good couple of minutes, it came to us. Oh! Remember the Sabbath and keep it holy! The Sabbath. For the life of us, none could remember the Sabbath. We can't seem to wrap our heads around just stopping. Stopping to simply be with each other. We obviously haven't placed a high enough value on this thing God wrote with his own finger on a stone tablet.

I was thinking recently about the days before cancer, before our circumstances brought us to the point where we chewed off every nail and challenged every medical and spiritual ideology. Before we landed in a foreign country searching for the meaning of life. Were we concerned then about stopping to enjoy what's here and now? Were we concerned then about keeping the Sabbath?

I got my answer while looking at old photos from the early days of our busy and important adulthood. We were so caught up working and meeting all the needs, we had neglected to take any breaks and had stopped doing most of the things we loved. I'd never seen us looking so pale and unhealthy. We took on the burden of adult life, of a new family of churches, of parenthood, and had subconsciously felt guilty about even the thought of making time for enjoying the things that were wired into us. Play, surfing, beach time, exercise, activities just for the sake of fun. We thought we were being super holy, that self-denial of anything superfluous and trivial like the beach would somehow rack up brownie points with God and Jesus. We couldn't have been more wrong.

Sabbath is a commandment. Rest, togetherness, celebration, fun. We have been biblically mandated to take a load off, to let God take over for a day. Blessings, presence, food, reflection, all have been prescribed to us—a people who would rather overdo it, who would try and take the credit. It's crazy that party time with God and loved ones happens to be a biblical mandate.

Sabbath looks different for everyone. For some, it's dinner with friends and a day of no obligations, maybe a nap or a family movie. For others it's playing hard, enjoying life-giving activities. It's clearing some margin. It's making time and space to be with each other. It's freely enjoying God's gifts of food, rest, and recreation. But the heart of the matter is the same. It's leaving our work and striving for God to worry about for a day, knowing that it's not we who hold the earth in the balance, but him. It's trading the unhealthy illusion of control and the addiction of distraction for the beneficial gift of presence. It's giving up the hustle and having confidence God will take care of things while we take a break.

Our decision to go off the grid in Israel served us well because it brought us into the right here, right now—ushered us into a lifestyle of Sabbath. It gave us space from the noise, gave us the luxury of distraction-free living. It had a way of scrubbing off the film that had grown over the heart of real life so that we could see each other up close. It gave us our breath back so that we could run our race with focus, and it was a chance to push the reset button and figure out what we wanted most out of life. When we talk about fewer choices and opting out, it can feel like deprivation. But it's just the opposite: it's abundance. The dichotomy is that it gives rather than takes.

How is God ushering you into Sabbath? Where might he be calling you to unplug? Is it turning your phone off one day a week? Is it daily making time for quiet, for family? Is it putting email in its place or only working during specific time slots or maybe turning off your wifi during certain hours? Perhaps it's more of a heart issue, trusting God to take care of all life's busy worries, or getting a clear view on how much connectivity is spiritually and emotionally healthy.

Because there's a lot of other things to say yes to, a lot in this beautiful world to see. And maybe, just maybe, God is calling you to stop and smell the shawarma.

four

A BAD CASE OF FOMO

So, I have a confession: I'm a homeschool mom. Yes, I know, we have a certain *je ne sais quoi* about us, and it's not always the good kind. Homeschool moms are a quirky bunch, and honestly, before I made the choice to quit traditional school, I didn't really want to be associated with the stereotype, whether it was my kids' reputation or my own. Come on, you know what I'm talking about: no-shoe-wearing, shaggy-haired kids who play obscure instruments. Or little girls obsessed with the pioneer days of American history. And the moms? We're even worse. We get giddy about model volcanoes made with baking soda and vinegar and talk for hours about curriculum. Boring.

Okay, so here's another confession: it's not as painfully nerdy as it seems, and now I am actually pretty proud of our lifestyle choice. We hang at the beach, we surf with our kids, we travel and cook and hike and camp and let it all count as science or a field trip. Our kids get hunting licenses at age twelve (okay, maybe my son is the exception in our blue state), paying jobs at age fourteen, and start their own businesses at age seventeen.

Yes, I'm painting a dreamy picture, but only for some. Because let's be honest about the whole thing, and let me tell you what a more seasoned mom told me before I got started: The greatest part of homeschooling is that your kids are with you all the time. And the worst thing about homeschooling is that your kids are with you *all the time.* Gosh, I need some space just typing that sentence. Being *with* people, all the time. I'm not just talking homeschooling now; I'm talking real life. Being with *your* people, the ones who let it all hang out, the ones who call you mom or wife or sister or daughter or friend. Being *with* is not always a picnic. In fact, it's exhausting.

Maybe that's why we have a hard time being present with those who occupy our immediate space, why it's so uncomfortable and unsavory. Maybe it's because we see each other's shortcomings in full view, are forced to deal with each other's endless issues, wearing us down and tiring us out, tempting us to reach out to the noncommittal virtual world—our online people happen to be a lot less needy and a lot less annoying. But it's the people God put around us who deserve our first fruits and our best, not strangers. That's where the struggle comes in—the nitty-gritty of doing life with those who see our flaws and who are flawed themselves. It's not very glamorous work.

In the online world, no one will ask us to make them a sandwich; they won't drop crumbs on the floor. They won't ask you to wipe their bottom or wash their karate uniform or give them a ride downtown. Our online communities are cheap dates, sources of constant affirmation without having to work very hard for it. But they also won't hold your hand while you wait for the diagnosis. They won't bring you chicken soup or lend you maternity clothes. They won't look in your eyes and ask what's on your mind or watch your kids while you get your roots touched up. They can't hug you when you are sad, don't know your favorite foods, and won't call you out when you are in sin. They won't know just by your body language that you need prayer or witness the way you really talk to your husband or kids. The actual, tangible people in our lives are priceless.

But I think the myth of the cool kids never goes away. Our world is such that we want to worship other people, fancy people, those with showy gifts or magnetic beauty. We secretly hope these people want us in their in-crowd, that they would be our best friends if they just knew us. Our actual people start to look shabby, so we start to look to the people we see on a screen. I'm totally guilty of that. I think it's that same line of thinking that sparks inclinations toward adultery. *If only I could be with someone else. My person is just so flawed.* News flash: we are all flawed, and no one person or social circle or movement is going to turn our flawed little lives into perfection.

I vote we stop looking to online personas to make our lives amazing and start investing in our own people, our quirky bands of girlfriends. Let's invest in our own imperfect marriages, our own messy kids. Let's get other people off the pedestal and admit that they have issues too. Because those we idolize—that girl on Instagram who has it all together, that speaker who is so dynamic and powerful—they put their pants on one leg at a time, they get the stomach flu, they get grumpy and jealous and anxious, just like us. They get impatient in long lines and spill coffee on their favorite shirts. They lose it when their kids bicker; they wish their pants zipped up without a fight. Those fancy, perfect, #goals people burn the toast, shop the bargain aisles at Target, plug up the toilet, and get their unibrows waxed. And you know what else? They have secret sins, just like the rest of us, things they are embarrassed to admit, problems they are working out, habits and fears and obsessions and insecurities. Let's not be so quick to trade one brand of crazy for another; it's never a good deal.

How do we separate reality from fantasy? What can we do to invest in our here-and-now people? I think you might know where I'm going with this, and you're either getting ready to fist-bump me or toss me out with the recycling. Please know that I'm going into this conversation without judgment. No finger-pointing, no hellfire. I'm definitely not any holier than you. And maybe, just maybe, you'll feel a little freer after we discuss it, so here goes: Let's talk about Instagram for a minute. Or like a hundred minutes. I don't know a single woman who is so free and healthy when it comes to Instagram that scrolling through has never stirred up either envy, anger, self-righteousness, or self-pity within her. Instagram is the strangest blend of inspiration and influence and inclusion while at the same time fueling covetousness and conceit. The constant feed of Things That Are Not Yours—boyfriends, babies, beautiful homes, abs of steel, amazing vacations, artsy abilities—begins to grate.

We think if we publish all our coolest moments, if we gather friends and followers, we will matter more, feel more important, more wanted. But that's not true; it's just a facade. The affirmation and attention of strangers is no substitute for the people who really know us. I learned through experience that when we set social media aside, it forces us to look at who is in our true inner circle. Who are the people closest to me whom I'd like to share my moments with? When we reprioritize our relationships, the ones actually with us are the ones who matter, and the shared moments become more meaningful.

Something happened on the way to Israel that shed some light on the flimsy veneer of social media from a firsthand perspective. We had stopped in Boston for a few days to visit dear friends of ours who moved from California to plant a church. One gorgeous afternoon, our families enjoyed a lazy picnic in the Arnold Arboretum. The flora was lush and vibrant, our four collective little girls were running free, and we lounged on a blanket, laughing and crying with our intimate, precious friends. My friend Nina took a picture of the scene and posted it on Instagram, and it really was a gorgeous post. It looked like the perfect day, perfect families, perfect charcuterie board. I almost felt jealous looking at our own picture. But then I knew what our reality was. We were two desperately troubled families, both deep in sorrow for different reasons: one on our way to another country to try and save our daughter's life, and the other feeling pressed down and strangled by depression and spiritual warfare in the deep work of church planting. We weren't two perfect families; we were two families struggling for breath.

Things are not always as they seem.

Sometimes it's hard to remember the divide between what's real and what's fiction. What's in theory and what's in practice. They're two completely different things, and when we don't look up, we can find ourselves walking on the wrong side of the road. My first inkling that something was amiss with my balance and perspective of social media came when we were at the hospital in UCLA harvesting Daisy's stem cells in preparation for her treatments. I was slumped in a slick artificial leather chair by the window. The view was solid concrete in every direction. I had Instagram open on my phone, and I sat scrolling through all my friends' online lives, only seeing the huge divide between theirs and mine. My little girl lay in the sterile hospital bed, bald and listless, while my friends' children frolicked on the beach, long tresses blowing in the fresh air. I scrolled and scrolled while the envy grew more insatiable, and all the while, Daisy languished. I finally felt the nudge from God. *Look up. Look up from your screen, and see what you have. Daisy's still here, and she's as lovely as ever. She is darling and funny and needs your attention. She's all yours, no one else's. For the love, woman, look up.*

Coming out of my Insta-stupor I saw her face, how she made room for me in her hospital bed, patting the sheet beside her. I saw the way she invited me to do puzzles while we listened to music, how she would scrunch up her nose when she beat me at cards. I saw the way she craved my full attention, how fortunate I was to be in the room with her, and right then something changed between me and social media. I knew that staying on it the way I had been doing would compel me to be anything but present; it would foster anything but contentment. And I knew I didn't want to waste another second of our time together on it. So, I cut it off. I deleted the app from my phone and made sure to forget my password.

I saw how ridiculous a choice it would have been for me to stay on Instagram when we left for Israel. Can you imagine all the gauche photo ops? *Here's Daisy on the Sea of Galilee! Walk on water, girl! (winky face emoji)* Or, *Guess who's at Abu Hassan?! Hummus for days!* (You actually do need to go there next time you're in Israel. It's like the Middle Eastern In-N-Out.) *Looking good in Jaffa. Where's Jonah? (whale emoji) At the Wailing Wall, y'all! (praying hands emoji) Walking the Via Dolorosa. Carry that cross, Daisy!* You get the idea. I couldn't imagine cheapening our experience by inviting the public into our most intimate and numbered days. I didn't want to miss a minute of our real lives choosing filters, making sure my best side was showing, or coming up with cheeky captions, not to mention the time spent reading comments. And you know what a split second's attention people give to other people's photos, right? We weren't about to lay out our most precious moments to be hastily double-tapped before people scrolled onward. *I'm so glad I took the time out of this intimate family moment so that you can move your eyebrows up a hair and grunt when your eyes flicker over my most precious loved ones. Hey, people. I'm here for you.*

Needless to say, I have never regretted that decision. Eliminating the risk of missing golden moments because of spending too much time sharing wasn't the only benefit. In addition to the freedom from the pressure to perform, I also noticed that I really enjoyed not knowing everyone else's business. It released me to be myself, to like what I want to like, and it cultivated contentment just by getting rid of comparison. But the best part about opting out of Instagram was the way I got to experience beautiful moments in their fullness, just me and whoever I was in the company of, not spread thin over cyberspace. Because contrary to the popular belief that if you didn't post it on Insta it didn't happen, gorgeous moments present themselves continually. And they're pretty delicious when unshared.

❋

It seems more and more, as we live in the digital age, there is a counterfeit for every real thing. We stare at screens instead of looking out windows at meadows and mountains. We envy other people's pictures, though they're often filtered and angled so they portray something that isn't genuine. We prefer to send emojis and text rather than talk face-to-face. In fact, just this morning, I was talking to a friend and making plans for our families to camp in Baja. He remembered Britt uses a flip phone, so he asked me if Britt texts. When I told him he'd have to call, he said, "Nope, I don't call people. That's way too intimate." He wasn't kidding.

Since when did the phone become so intimate? Remember when a phone call was like copping out? It used to be considered distant and impersonal to only have phone conversations and never face-to-face. Now it's a feared thing, bordering on inappropriate. Like, *I can't believe she called me. What does she think, we're related by blood or something?* Just recently I made a new acquaintance at a dinner party, and after chatting and bonding over shared experiences for two hours, I handed her my phone so she could enter her number. She paused and stared incredulously at the phone like I had just asked to borrow her underwear, then reluctantly put her info in. After that reaction, I decided I wouldn't be calling. Or even texting. Apparently, connecting privately and not on social media has become uncomfortably close.

Oddly enough, with the whole world invited into your business, it's social media that feels uncomfortably close to me, but in a noncommittal way. One of the deepest issues with social media is that it creates a false sense of connection. It affords people privileges into other people's lives that usually only close friends are allowed, yet without the loyalty and responsibility of true relationship. We can now see inside people's homes without being invited, witness their vacations and Christmas mornings and children's milestones, all without the commitment of getting in the car and bringing a salad, changing each other's kids' diapers, or helping each other move to new homes.

We get the affirmation boost and the warm fuzzies of compliments when we post, and we get to feel relational when we comment, but these things are a shabby substitute for actual, real community. Actual, real community is far more than a shout-out. Actual, real community is far richer in relationship. It means you laugh together till your abs are sore; it means you cry together till your mascara's gone. It means your dearest friends will see you in your shabbiest clothes eating ice cream straight from the carton on the floor of your kitchen and still love you, that your baby will throw up on their cashmere sweater and they won't bat an eye. It means you offend each other with misunderstandings and then hear each other out, hugging in the end. It means you fight hard in prayer for the things that never hit the highlight reel: the kids going sideways, the bank account being overdrawn, the medical scares. It means you borrow each other's clothes, that you exclaim, "You're rocking your new mom bod!"

with sincerity and congratulations; it means you squeeze your muffin top and make your belly button tell jokes while getting dressed together on a girls' trip. It's the real thing. Genuine and satisfying.

Actual, real community is a full plate, with the protein, the fiber, and the fat that goes deep and satisfies, while online "friends" can only offer a meal of Sour Patch Kids. Bright, sweet, and addicting, but in the end too much makes you sick. We can't survive on fake, friends. It's time to put our social media into submission. Let it be a fun side dish, not the full meal. Let it be a tool to share goodness, not to wallow in comparison. Let it enhance and supplement life, not rip it off. Take back your community; revisit your "friend" situation. Unfollow anyone who is causing you turmoil; unfollow anyone who makes you feel inferior. Post with care, and never post if it means interrupting a pure and glorious moment—it won't be worth it. Once you get the hang of it, contentment is allowed space to bloom. And you start to see that your life is pretty beautiful after all.

We need to be ruthless when it comes to things that inhibit presence in our face-to-face relationships. We need to ask why we hold each other at bay with screens and fingers flying over our tiny keyboards, creating whatever image we want to portray while we miss out on reality. What are we hiding from, and what is the result? Is there a better way, and if so, what is it? My family and I asked ourselves these questions when death was staring us in the face, but really, death is staring all of us in the face. None of us can afford to miss out on the real for the contrived: today is all any of us has.

What are the true ingredients of relational life, the ones that cause us to nourish and flourish? Can we go back to the things we've rid ourselves of in the name of efficiency, in the name of productivity? I'm talking the good old analog days of reading facial expressions and body language. Valuing quality over quantity in our friendships. Being okay with not seeing everything there is to see, not keeping up with the latest rumor or outrage or sound bite. Looking for the good and true and beautiful that's right in front of our faces.

Just the other day I lazily watched the sunset from my patio with my treasured best friend of a husband, feet propped up, head tipped back. The sun radiated gentle and kind on our faces while the neighbor's horses flicked their tails in the fading light. As we clinked glasses, I turned to him and said, "I'm so glad I'm not sharing this moment with anyone else." My moments are my own, and sharing can be limited to those closest to my heart. It's almost sacred.

✳

I've talked to a lot of people since my departure from social media. Many of them pull me aside and say they wish they could do the same, but that for some reason or other they just can't: work, family obligations, product promotion, or just plain FOMO (fear of missing out). In fact, I was recently listening to a podcast I love, on which I was also previously a guest. The woman being interviewed was talking about her love/hate relationship with Instagram and how she goes about keeping it in its place. She then mentioned that she'd heard an interview in which the person didn't even have social media (me). *Gasp!* The host said, "Yes, I know! And she's an author too!" The guest responded by saying she didn't remember that part, just that I had opted out of social. When I heard that, I was flabbergasted. My interview was about losing my daughter to cancer and writing a book about it, but the only thing she remembered from the hour-long conversation was my hiatus from Instagram. That spoke to her more than anything else, and it gave me a glimpse into how strong our collective case of FOMO is.

We've been bamboozled to believe that we would be missing out on something if we didn't see so-and-so's wedding pictures or know about such-and-such event. But what about missing out on our own people, our own events? How many times have you missed a good twenty minutes of something wonderful because you just *had* to share it online? And then later spent time worrying about what people thought of your post? Man, we have a bad case of FOMO, all right, but it's misdirected. Our FOMO needs to be pointed right back to ourselves. We are missing what's right in front of us, and that should freak us out.

Now, this is what I'm not saying: I'm not saying social media is evil and no one should participate. I'm not saying that it's worthless or shallow or altogether detrimental to our health. I'm not saying there is nothing good that comes from using social media, that friendships shouldn't be formed unless they're in person. I'm not saying that there isn't encouragement or inspiration or truth or beauty to be found. I'm not saying you should delete all forms of it from your life right this minute or that every person reading this has a major problem.

This is what I am saying: if and when we choose to participate, we must master it so it doesn't master us. I'm saying we should never choose a screen over a real live person. I'm saying we need to be completely aware that it is no substitute for reality, that filters and angles and captions do not a real life make. Keep an eye on how it makes you feel, what it stirs up in you. Never use it to satisfy your need for affirmation or significance. Let's use the moments of our lives to build up something in the flesh as often as we are able, and consider our online people as secondary.

You do have a choice in the matter. You don't have to spend time and energy on people and photos that make your blood boil with anger, that make you feel small, that make you feel ugly or lame, that distract you from the most important people and adventures in your life. You have a choice in how you will let FOMO serve you: Will you fear missing out on other people's lives, or will you fear missing out on your own?

If I ever go back on Instagram, it will be with eyes wide open. It will be to encourage or be encouraged. It will be to inspire or be inspired. It will be kept in its place, never usurping what's real and right in front of me. It will be in the flow of my actual life, not damming up the good, true, and beautiful mess of the human experience with its shiny pixels. I'm not sure if I ever will pick it back up again, but if I do, it will be with a healthy, well-directed FOMO.

five

KNOCKED OFF MY HIGH HORSE

When we were getting settled in Israel, having fewer distractions and becoming truly hands-free for the first time in years, our perceptions were sharpened to what was happening around us. It was like that weird phenomenon that occurs when you watch a documentary and become informed and all of a sudden you feel superior. You walk around itching to evangelize about the dangers of GMOs, or the political hold on American farming, or the devastation of fast fashion. Maybe you've read a few books on parenting, and now every other kid you see out in public is a hideous brat, and *Lady, how can you be so blind? How do you not see your kid is a future convict?* We love to feel like we have the corner on whatever it is we deem important. Or perhaps, as in my case, it's more about what you're suddenly super holy about.

Soon after going off the grid, I was that super holy, judgy girl, neck sore from shaking my head at every person who was looking at their phone. And, honestly, the people of Israel were at least as phone-addicted as Americans, perhaps more so. We noticed that most people in cafés would sit down across from each other placing their phones face up, parallel with the knife and spoon—a welcome guest. I was surprised they didn't get menus for their phones, they gave them so much prominence. As the four of us would sit down and go about our meal, we would look around and tsk-tsk the others. Shaking our heads, we would pull out our deck of cards, because unlike all these freaks, we actually *talk* to each other, we are *relating* to each other. We actually *know* how to have a civilized meal. The shuffling would commence, the teasing about who's winning at our favorite card game (it's called Chance; I highly recommend it) as we self-righteously enjoyed our haloumi sandwiches or vegan burritos. *We are so present right now*, I would say to myself, superior and virtuous. *I'm so glad we are not like those sinners with the phones.*

Yes, we were the most present people in Israel. Right there, in our little family bubble. Safely separate. Wholly holy. But, soon enough, we started to meet people who challenged our assumptions, whose actions showed us there's more to practicing presence than merely unplugging. Beautiful people, different people. People who served our lunches, people who administered medical treatment, people we rented apartments from, people we met at the juice stand, and I began to be proven wrong about the population of Israel and their apparent lack of presence. What I saw instead was an invitation into fellowship, and I wanted a piece of it.

I began to look out for their habits of being that ushered us in. I knew there was a common thread; it just took a bit to see it. But that's part of the journey, isn't it? Picking up the bread crumbs of goodness, leading the way to higher ground. The bread crumbs each looked slightly different but had the same substance. With-ness. In Israel, we got a glimpse of the various ways *with-ness* looks—what it is to be present with the people in your space—and it turns out it looked a little bit different than I thought, a little bit out of our comfort zone. Different and uncomfortable, yes, but life-giving and lovely.

✳

August 2012 was blazing hot in the Holy Land. The land, sea, and air all set at the same temperature: inferno. It would be a month or so before the weather shifted into the sweet balmy stage that comes before the winter rains and chill set in. The first chance we had away from the clinic in the afternoon, we headed down to the beach. After endlessly searching the impossible metropolitan parking situation, we found a beach with a parking lot just outside the city of Tel Aviv. We discovered that, for a small fee, you could enjoy this pretty beach that boasted morning trash pickup service, which is totally my tree-hugging love language. Boom, we had found our new hangout. It was called Ha Tzuk, meaning "the cliff," and looked a lot like our favorite beach in California. Beaches feel like home to us, since all four of us grew up on one. We were excited to feel a little like we belonged, like we could, for a few hours, forget that we were foreigners and fighting a cancer that would not submit.

At first, we felt wobbly and unsettled in Israel, still getting over jet lag, still getting oriented. Our core sense as a family was loneliness. Fear. Being an outsider. All around us wherever we went, we heard chatter in a language that wasn't ours to speak. I remember sitting on that beach, sun going down, the heat persisting like a fever that refuses to break. I wondered if there would ever be a change in the weather. In us. Could we survive these next few months? The longer we spent at the beach, the heavier I felt. I looked around at the trash left on the ground waiting to be picked up, wrappers printed in words and symbols I couldn't read, the bubbling of language all around me, indecipherable and exclusive. I felt the temperature, the way it was dense and static, not dropping after the sun disappeared. I saw the way my thin, sick little girl lay on her towel, brave on an international quest for a cure. I looked out on the water, the way the wind swept up and brought waves with it, how those waves alternated gold in the reflection of the setting sun and glittering black in the shadows.

I felt alone. I felt detached. I felt uncomfortable. And then he walked up.

A bald man, perhaps five or so years older than my husband. He had a kind face and the distinctive athletic Israeli look we saw all over the beach. As he picked his way through the beachgoers and over the sand, he held two popsicles. One for Daisy, one for Isaiah. My little girl's freckled face lit up, my son's smile shone white in the fading daylight, and for that moment, we felt like we belonged. He didn't say much, just "for you," or something along those lines, along with a meaningful smile. But he looked us in the eye. He saw us. And we experienced something different, something healing. The exit from one person's comfort zone into another's.

The exchange ushered in awareness of a fellowship we were being invited into, and we started seeing the little ways we felt connected. Little gestures that made us feel *with* rather than *alone*. The attention this stranger paid us felt like a nod from God. It said, *I see you. We are here together,* and we loved it. The man with the popsicles was the first of multiple moments of connection, of with-ness. It was not only emotionally healing and stirred up courage, but it taught us much: about not merely setting aside distractions but putting forth the effort to connect, holding another's gaze, and being right here, right now. With.

One mild Shabbat evening, the kind when the sky slips into a lovely shade of lavender and the air settles on your skin like cashmere, the four of us were out for a walk around the neighborhood together. We were staying in a town called Zichron Ya'acov, which has been called the "Israeli Provence" for its wineries, country feel, and pedestrian street draped with swooping Italian lights. It was a smallish town, situated on a mesa-like hill above Caesarea, which is right on the Mediterranean Sea. The neighborhood we stayed in was adjacent to a nature reserve, and we loved to wander the streets and trails as often as we could when we weren't in Tel Aviv getting Daisy's treatment.

On that particular walk, we were admiring a few really stunning modern houses in the nicer section of the neighborhood. We were slowly ambling down the street, discussing all the things we liked about a particularly swanky home, when we saw her. She stood on the upstairs balcony wrapped in a bathrobe, wet hair shoulder length and combed straight back. She had a glass of red wine in her hand and was looking down at us.

"Hey!" she shouted, before we could get out from under her stare. Shocked and slightly embarrassed, we waved and shuffled on to make it look like we weren't just caught dissecting every aspect of her gorgeous home. We nodded and smiled, and like most Americans do, feigned busy so that we could get out of taking the relationship a step further. But this freshly showered woman stepped right out of her comfort zone and right into ours.

"Hey, are you Americans?" she loudly asked, wine threatening to splash over the rim, robe making each of us secretly uncomfortable as we wondered if she was perhaps a bit touched in the head. But we swallowed our misgivings and answered her question, striking up an awkward conversation right there—she on the balcony like Juliet and us on the sidewalk like an odd bunch of desperate suitors. After a minute or so she invited us in, and while exchanging questioning looks among ourselves, we agreed.

It turned out she was an American Jew from Baltimore who married an Orthodox Jew from Zurich, and they both made Aliyah (the immigration of Jews from the diaspora to the land of Israel—literally "the act of going up" to Jerusalem). She explained that her husband and children were at shul observing Shabbat evening service, and she was relaxing and waiting to have dinner with them after having made all her preparations before sundown. She showed us around her amazing house, chattered on about her children who happened to be close in age with mine, and extended an invitation to use her pool anytime.

We ended up becoming friends in the weeks we stayed in that neighborhood, and through her openness, I learned much about the Orthodox community from her conversion perspective. While our kids played, she told me all about Shabbat, about synagogue, about Jewish family life. She gave me a key to her gate so we could swim when she wasn't there, and she showed us what it looks like to love your actual neighbor. Not only did I learn much about her and her people, our friendship showed me a thing or two about myself, taught me the value of taking a step further into fellowship even when it's uncomfortable.

I'll admit, first impressions are the most long-lasting, and even though we will always refer to her as the lady in the bathrobe with the wine—still totally cringeworthy— she was a genuine example of Israeli hospitality: making someone feel known by giving them your full attention, and spontaneously inviting someone into your space whether or not you have it all together (or even all your clothes on). She was just one of many who invited us into their presence, who gave of their time and attention, who taught us a thing or two about what it is to be *with*. And even with all the things we were learning about unplugging, all the ways we were stopping to smell the shawarma, we had a thing or two to learn about opening our hearts, about the invitation of strangers, about seeing and being seen.

＊

In the days following, we witnessed more beautifully original actions that gave us the present, life-giving human connection we so thirsted for. Getting out of our comfort zone was definitely the first thing we were taught, but right up there with that was more of a tangible expression we eventually caught on to. I first noticed that connection, one of heart to hand, in a teeny surfboard factory in Jaffa.

We had an Israeli friend named Hani (whom we'd met in California a few years before) who designed, built, and sold surfboards. He and his family were kind, loving, and super cool, and we looked forward to meeting up on his turf. Hani's factory and shop were a few blocks from the famous port where an unruly Jonah once hopped a ship to Tarshish. Beyond the cobblestone streets and ancient stone buildings were larger, more modern versions of Israeli architecture: straight lines, boxy cement apartment buildings with businesses on the first floor and living quarters above, and lots of visible rebar. Searching for the factory felt like exploring the moon—a dusty, pale landscape with craters of all sizes strewn about. We carefully wound our way through the alleys, vigilant not to plunge our flip-flopped feet into the stinky muck-filled potholes.

Jaffa is sketchy, minus the romantic historical part, so I held Daisy's hand tightly and chose to admire the colorful graffiti-laden walls instead of overthinking it. We finally arrived at our destination, which was marked by a few schlocky motorcycles and various junky cars. It was the typical Israeli building: half-finished yet boasting the indispensable bomb shelter. Outside the door of the shop there were barrels of resin for glassing boards—fat drips dried in long waxlike layers down the sides—dumpsters overflowing with fiberglass cloth, foam dust, and piles of the quintessential unidentified stickiness that adorns surfboard factories. Basically, not the most tidy of atmospheres, but we knew we were in the right place.

I was used to surfboard factories, seeing as my

husband worked in one, but this was next level. We entered the space, which, while super disheveled, was also super cool. It was set up like any other hardcore surf shop, complete with all the gear an Israeli surfer would need. There were racks of board leashes looped like licorice, stacks of traction pads, rows of board bags hanging like curtains, and a small offering of board shorts. In the middle of the shop stood a couple of dirty couches, a rattan chair, and a smudged coffee table strewn with surf magazines. And, like in most surf shops, there were only dudes inside. Scruffy, sunburned guys, all with the universal surfer stance: shoulders thrown back, chest out, simultaneously strong and easygoing. But, again, dudes. Dudes speaking Hebrew in a rough neighborhood. I wasn't expecting a whole lot of connection or presence from this rugged bunch.

As we walked in to say hello, the tallest, scruffiest guy met us at the door. Redheaded and lanky (and likely the only ginger in all of Israel), he greeted us warmly and looked us in the eye. Then he did something that cultivated with-ness in the most profound way: he pulled out a warm liter of Coke and a package of Flaky Flix cookies. The waffle-crisp kind, in two flavors—strawberry and vanilla. He threw them down on the coffee table with an air of gladness and offered us a place to sit, gesturing to the couches with a sweep of his hand. There we talked and laughed and, as we carefully bit the tops off the wafers and licked the pink cream filling, we felt welcomed. The food offering became the invitation into his world, the invitation to relate, the seeing and being seen. Without words it said, *I see you. Let's be together. Let's have a treat and stop what we're doing to connect.*

We spent time in the factory that day, time that others considered worth spending on us. We made new friends, had a few laughs, and left feeling refreshed. We felt the joy of entering into what and who was right in front of us. The daunting walk back through Jaffa's crowded streets saturated with crazy drivers and broken glass was a little less exhausting than it had been earlier, a little less stressful. Our loneliness had been lifted a bit, with just a taste of Coke, cookies, and tanned friendly faces.

Not long after we enjoyed our sugar rush with the guys in Hani's factory, we met with a woman and her husband up in Caesarea. We had found her on VRBO and were hoping to rent her apartment for a while, as we had limited time at our first landing place. We piled in the car and drove to the teeny house, which happened to be the couple's vacation home. We entered the place, modern and compact, and with the six of us in the living room, there was barely space to breathe. It's not the most agreeable thing, being stuck in such close quarters with complete strangers. Talk about comfort zones—mine was being invaded big-time.

After showing us the place (which took about fifteen seconds), there was that moment of awkward silence we all dread, everyone standing around nodding like dashboard bobble heads. Suddenly the owner began opening her cupboards and searching. For what, I didn't know. After a minute, she triumphantly held up a crinkly, colorful bag with little cartoon characters on it. Marshmallows. There was nothing in the entire kitchen except a bag of marshmallows. Like the waffle cookies, they were pink and white and looked like play food you'd find in a child's make-believe kitchen. Neither fear of discomfort nor pressure of perfection stopped this woman from offering us a bit of herself. She ripped that bag of marshmallows open right there on the table that seated only four and proceeded to give us all her attention while we were entertained by the slightly comical act of eating pink marshmallows with complete strangers.

We talked and laughed, and strangers became friends that day. The marshmallows were a manifestation of a habit of being, a way to be present with someone that says *right now you're my priority*. A habit that teaches us to look into one another's eyes rather than over each other's shoulder for someone better to talk to. A habit that reminds the people you are with that you are together. And that they are worth your time.

None of these people had anything fancy to offer, but it was the habit of offering what they *did* have that made the difference. It was an offering of with-ness, for at least as long as it took to eat the snacks or hand over the pool key. It was an offering of vulnerability, an openness to bring someone else into your world no matter the imperfection. Fear of judgment wasn't on the radar, only the joy of togetherness.

✳

I'm pretty sure God is in the ethos of face-to-face connection. I see it in the way he's designed family and the body of Christ. Life is not meant to be done alone, but we are to laugh and weep and break bread together. He designed us with needs to be met in community and to meet others right there in that need. He offers ways of creating habits to draw us closer to himself and to others; we just need to be open to it right where we are, whether we are in our bathrobes, whether the Coke is warm, and whether the setting is splendid or squalid. Those moments of with-ness we experienced in Israel resulted in delightful fellowship. We ended up becoming friends with the popsicle man. We had him to our apartment to play cards; we took him out to dinner. We spent Rosh Hashanah with Hani's family in Jaffa, happily squished in his dad's tiny apartment, seated at a table piled up with tasty traditional Israeli food, surrounded by a boisterous Jewish family. And we learned to extend what we had to offer. Just like wine lady extended her home to us, rental lady offered pink marshmallows, and surf shop guy presented us with Flaky Flix and Coke, we remembered we had something we could share.

Back in California, while packing for the trip, we had loaded up a bag with Channel Islands goods to share with local surfers, knowing surf gear is somewhat scarce in that part of the world. We had leashes, deck pads, stickers, and a few tee shirts. Since we were surfing at Ha Tzuk daily after Daisy's treatment, we usually saw the same guys out in the water. One by one, we gave them our gifts. And even with the language and culture barrier, whenever we approached a guy and told him we had brought some cool stuff with us from America, we watched dark eyes light up and enjoyed the bright, infectious smiles of sun-whitened teeth. Being with these guys and giving what we had delighted us. It became one of the most fun things we could do: go make a new friend on the beach, give a gift from California, and feel a bit less overwhelmed by our circumstances.

It was not enough for us to lay our phones down, to simply disconnect from our hectic lifestyle, on the search for true and real fellowship. We had to take it a step further, to find a deeper level of openness to the faces in front of us, and it took initiation toward the community we found ourselves in. We learned a lot from our new friends and their style of togetherness. The initiating and giving rather than isolating and defending. The accepting rather than judging. We learned to embrace those things and make them a part of our own habit of being, a path to presence that changed our perspective. Putting the phone down is a start, yes, but moving out of the comfort zone is another. The thought that I had presence nailed, that going off the grid was the ultimate, most present thing to do, was quickly disproved. I got knocked off my high horse, I did. And I'm grateful.

six

CRISSCROSS APPLESAUCE

Recently I saw a minivan with the statement "Kids are like farts; you can only stand your own" boldly emblazoned in white paint on the rear window. I mean, who does that? And while the initial imagery of this vulgar pronouncement might make us cringe, my usual reaction would be to say how true it is with a chuckle. But today I find myself wanting to challenge the generosity of such words. I love being a mom and I adore my children, but, honestly, the content-o-meter in my home lately has been dipping into the red. This week I have contemplated Child Protective Services call–worthy acts, such as binding and gagging Fifi, who chatters and touches me incessantly, allowing Isaiah's bathroom to continue its current existence as a petri dish just to make a statement, and piling up all the dishes and toys and tchotchkes that seem to multiply in the night and lighting a match to them. Poof, gone. That last one I thought about more than once.

Kids actively test our every last nerve, bouncing up and down on them, stretching the weak spots until they snap clean through. They know just what buttons to push and have insider knowledge on what gets under our skin—figuratively and literally. Fifi likes to reach up under my shirt, grab my stomach with both hands, and smash it all around, saying, "Squishy, squishy," like she's talking to a sweet chubby baby. Isaiah knows just how to narrow his eyes at me, as if I'm an unpalatable, greasy creature who should never be let out in public. Fifi's daily routine is to crawl into my bed at 5:30 a.m. and crow like a rooster. "Dock-ta-loo-loo!" she says, self-satisfied. She crows again and again, until I haul my forty-three-year-old self out of bed and start the day.

When I first started having kids in my midtwenties, I said goodbye to a lot of things I loved to do. Finding myself surrounded by diapers and dirty laundry and feeling the burn of my newfound loss of freedom, I comforted myself by calculating that by the time I was in my early forties it would be *game on* for me. I would have one kid graduated from high school and the other almost there, so I would finally do all the things I had missed while taking care of littles: surfing, traveling, and the ever-luxurious going to the bathroom alone. I had my boy and my girl, wham bam. Having more was not on my radar. I was not about to start from scratch when I was on the home stretch. I was not about to go back into the world of sleep training, boogers, and cutting someone else's meat. Only freaks and fruitcakes start over with babies when they're almost home free.

Then Fifi arrived.

What happened to my glamorous plans of living the dream in my forties? I was supposed to be surfing all day or jetting off to Spain, not standing at the kitchen counter haggardly eating my breakfast in my saggy, stained bathrobe. After all these years of being a mom, I've lost all sense of personal dignity and anything resembling youthful energetic freshness. I guess I shouldn't be surprised, seeing as motherhood begins with pregnancy, and pregnancy with nausea. As the wise say, the struggle is real.

But honestly, I'm embarrassed at my attitude toward Fifi sometimes. Her given name is Pheodora. It's Greek for "supreme gift," and God gave her to me just over a year after I said my last goodbyes to Daisy. So why am I so shortsighted? How is it that I can know for a fact she is straight from the generosity of God and yet carry around this gross attitude, only focusing on the harder, more tedious parts? Why do I continually forget she is a privilege and gift not afforded to every woman? Why do I complain about the drudgery, yet miss the way her fingers feel on the back of my neck when she hugs me? Why do I groan about the unglamorous reality of toddlers, yet completely overlook the fact that she's full of joie de vivre and fills my near-empty home with the song of love? How have I gotten so complacent with God's generosity toward me that I'm acting this way?

It sounds embarrassing when I lay it out like this. Dissatisfaction has never looked good on me.

Today, as I write this, I am the most discontent person in the whole tri-county area. Well, at least in a one-mile radius. Since I woke up (with Fifi in my bed, bouncing on my bladder and licking my face with her morning breath), I've felt lonely, bored, depressed. I've felt like throwing in the towel on motherhood, because the patience I've been so famous for in the past years of caring for Daisy has left the building. All day long I've resented my life as stay-home homeschooling mom while juggling a writing career. I keep turning the manuscript deadline over and over in my head, wondering how on earth I'm going to do it all. I've spent the morning picking up toys, vacuuming, making and cleaning up food, correcting my son's English essay, cleaning out the chicken coop, playing "surfing ponies," "luchadores" (Google it), and "renchrant" (restaurant). Finally, at 1:00 p.m., Fifi went down for a nap after asking for another snack, another story, and another kiss. I'm tapped out, but now it's time to work.

I am writing this entire book at naptime. Actually, I wrote my last book at naptime, too, but that one was about joy in suffering, not presence and contentment, so there was less temptation to complain. This time around I'm so hyperaware of each distraction, each discontented thought. I'm so overwhelmed by all the big and small tasks looming, all the things I have to do to keep a household going, a book written, and kids educated and loved. I want to check out; I want to scrap it all. I want to shop online or text a friend or drown my sorrows in chocolate, but I know they would be temporary answers to a deeper question.

So, before I sat down and opened up the computer, and while feeling fragile and on the verge of tears, I took some necessary steps to come out of my funk. I braided my hair. I put on some mascara. I changed out of my pajamas. And then I sat with someone who thinks I'm awesome, someone who thinks I'm lovely and smart, who was waiting around to love me and listen to me and speak to me. Someone who changed the whole course of the day with just a few words.

Jesus.

A bit of truth changed my whole trajectory. It was like the discontentment slid right off the plate and into the trash like leftover pizza crust: unappetizing and unnecessary. God's presence brought a little perspective, a little peace. That time spent with him was like visiting my new dermatologist, digging around to see what was causing my discontentment rash. As I sat with God, reading a bit of Mark and John and entering into the life of Jesus, he probed at my heart by introducing me to a new friend.

Mary of Bethany. Do you know her? She's probably most famous from the story of Mary and Martha, but she's also the Mary in the scandal of the expensive perfume she poured out on Jesus' feet. In the two accounts we see two sides of her, both seemingly extravagant and dreamy, both entirely radical. Mary embodies the journey of presence that brings her into contentment, her life an example of beautiful moments making up a beautiful whole.

Enter Mary and Martha's home with me. They were sisters from Bethany who had invited Jesus over for dinner. Now, when you invite Jesus, you also invite twelve of his best bros—and who knows how many others—as he always seemed to be surrounded by groupies and stragglers. Sounds like an ancient rock band, especially with all the hair and eccentric followers. Either way, there were at least sixteen for dinner, which is a substantial dinner party. I can just imagine all the disciples crammed into the room, dusty, sweaty, and disheveled. Jesus the miracle maker was the guest of honor, so there had to be a bit of fangirling going on, perhaps some "Can I take your cloak, Jesus?" "Freshly baked challah for you, Jesus?" Or "Jesus, your beard is looking fab!" There was definitely the splash of foot washing, perhaps the sleek drizzle of anointing oil on the head.

I love to entertain. I love lighting dozens of candles, cutting sprigs of lavender and rosemary for each plate. I love the platters stacked with dates and nuts and cheese, the varying heights of my thrift-store goblets and glasses. I love the festive vibe and the theme, whether it's wahoo tacos and mango salsa or grilled elk sausages with mustard and a huge lemony salad. I love serving and blessing friends in the form of food. And no one can argue that it's not an important use of time, because everyone loves the cook. The murmurs of *mmm* and *ooh, what's in this?* The hugs and thank-yous. Hosting is simultaneously artful, selfless, giving, creative, and results in a lot of affirmation, but it is also a ton of work beforehand. And it sounds to me like Martha and Mary's dinner party was impromptu. *Swing on by, Jesus! No, no problem at all!* And in all the hustle and bustle, I think Martha and Mary might've had differing expectations for the evening, divergent hopes of how they might best spend this time in Jesus' presence.

So, the house was bustling; there was loads to do. And Martha was sweating in the kitchen. We are told she was distracted by all her preparations. Distracted by the crucial job that would make or break the dinner party. I guess distraction isn't just a twenty-first-century problem after all. I mean, can you imagine the pressure? Jesus the *Messiah* having dinner at your place! Martha probably felt her reputation was on the line—definitely her pride, as she seemed like the kind of woman who would kill you before she shared her famous hummus recipe. Exasperation set in as she turned her focus onto Mary, perched so preciously at the Lord's feet.

I picture Mary sitting crisscross applesauce, her tunic making a homespun bowl shape between her knees. Perhaps there was a downy pet lamb nestled on her lap, or the bowl of lentils she was supposed to sort through looking for pebbles. Head covering slightly askew, a dreamy look on her face, she was in the zone. It was no one but her and Jesus, and they were tracking.

Slacker! Martha thought, shooting darts at her sister through bossy laser eyes and passive-aggressively banging pots and pans around. *She's nothing but a doe-eyed slacker!*

Martha's distraction and discontentment was such a contrast to Jesus and Mary's absolute peace and presence with each other. When Martha demanded that Jesus force Mary to help in the kitchen, criticizing Mary for costing them valuable dinner prep time, what did Jesus say about the whole sisterly squabble? "My dear Martha, you are worried and upset over all these details! There is only one thing worth being concerned about. *Mary has discovered it,* and it will not be taken away from her" (Luke 10:41–42, emphasis mine).

There are two things I noticed as I read this pithy yet meaningful story. First, Mary was criticized for her unconventional choice of sitting at Jesus' feet. She was seen as being unfair and lazy, and culturally inappropriate, rather than wise. Martha was distracted by "her many preparations," and since Mary didn't agree that those things were more important than the opportunity to sit with Jesus, it took boldness for her to choose well. That is a real thing for many of us. So much of the time we are trying to measure up to everyone around us; we are people pleasing and affirmation hungry. We often set aside what's most important to God for what's most important to those around us so that we can satisfy others' needs and earn their approval. It takes a bit of enlightenment to see the better way—which is so often right in front of us—and then courage to walk in it. I'm guessing Martha would've come at Mary with a rolling pin if Jesus hadn't intercepted her.

The other thing I noticed was that Mary had to discover the better thing; it didn't just land in her lap. I don't think we are naturally born with a propensity toward the deep work of presence. I mean, what kid has more attention span than a fruit fly? I think we are more prone to distraction, to heaping more on our plates and into our lives that isn't necessary. But Jesus shows us that the act of being present is *learned*. It is *discovered*. Mary learned presence; she learned stillness. She discovered what's important—Jesus wouldn't always be there with them—and Mary made her choice.

Like Mary, I'm also in a place of discovery. As I roll the thoughts around in my head like a bingo cage, the ones coming to the surface for inspection are beginning to paint a picture. What started as my desire to fix the symptoms of an overconnected and crowded lifestyle has become a search to uncover the root of the problem of presence—and how to confront it at that deeper level. I believe it's more than just putting our phones down, reducing distraction, and cutting back on obligations. I believe our longing for peace and meaning and investing in the better thing boils down to that simple picture of Mary sitting with Jesus. Because of her example, I'm learning to look at presence and contentment systemically rather than symptomatically.

My discontentment today wasn't because of the

tedious physical outpour of motherhood or the pressure of my writing career. It wasn't just the distraction of my many preparations: running a home, educating my kids, supporting my husband. Those were just my current circumstances and so happened to be the trigger. The symptoms of feeling haggard and depleted indicated a deeper question, a deeper longing rolling around in my heart: *Am I loved and wanted?* The question underlying my feeling lonely, unseen, and uninvited was, *Am I enough, am I important?* And the mounting pressure of turning my manuscript in on time while still being a good mom pointed to the deeper matter of, *Can I trust God with my life's work?*

The way we choose to engage with our current circumstances sometimes shows us what's underneath the surface. I was worried I would let someone down, that I wouldn't do my best work inside or outside the home. I was worried that I would disappoint someone who had expectations of me and they would think less of me. And I was concerned that I wouldn't be appreciated for all my efforts with my family, wanting to be seen and affirmed for all the continuous, mind-numbing menial labor. These were the root issues behind today's grumbling and complaining, behind my desire to escape rather than lean in. And these are the questions that haunt us all, I think, if we would take the time to see past the veneer.

So, I take a step outside my circumstances. I look for the things I missed, the things Martha would miss, the invaluable things that adorn today. And I remember to measure my worth not on whether or not I am applauded for my work, but on how loved I am by God. If I can deal with these underlying issues, I can invest in my mundane days of hard work with confidence, even with peace and contentment.

If I'm to build something meaningful of my days, I must go into the plainest, most ordinary, boring days with open eyes. If I'm to build a whole beautiful life out of the smallest of moments, then the regular days count the most. And when I ask God what I really get for all my hard work, that is where the Teacher in Ecclesiastes hits me most with the truth. I can't see the whole scope of God's work in my life, but there he is, working in all seasons. I'm only responsible for showing up to today, because that's what I've been given.

After I sit awhile at Jesus' feet, among the cracker crumbs and dust bunnies and plastic ponies, I hear his voice. He whispers of his love for me, that he sees me. He reminds me that my work is not in vain and that I'm raising future world-changers. He whispers that investing in life now, as boring and unsexy as it is, will reap benefits in the future. As he breathes life on me like Aslan breathed life on all of Narnia, he opens my eyes to Fifi's bouncing caramel curls. The way she runs across the lawn chasing the chickens, screaming with laughter in her magical fairy voice. He shows me how privileged I really am to be here with her. He reveals in captured snippets how much it matters that I'm there for Isaiah. How I'm sowing unbreakable things into his life that will never be taken, and that the time is short.

All the years Daisy was sick I learned to lean into the hard stuff. I was right there. I knew how crucial that was to our survival and, besides, I didn't want to miss a moment with her. But now that life is normal, now that the days seem to stretch on endlessly, it's more of a challenge. The needs are more muddied, less obvious. The sweet times are frequent now, less of a contrast than during our hard years, so I tend not to notice them. But they are no less valuable, no less numbered. It's a learning curve, these days. I'm learning I don't want to miss out.

It might be different for you. My own struggles vary on any given day. But the point is searching beneath the obvious. Digging for the problem and then welcoming the solution. Maybe that's what Mary was doing. Maybe the love and joy and wisdom Jesus was sharing trumped all her preparations, her need for affirmation, her short-sightedness, her search for meaning in lesser things.

Presence is more than showing up. It's more than making eye contact with your people or setting your phone down or practicing zen-like meditation. It's investing in your people, your current situation, your actual life, not the people or situation or life you wish you had. Presence insists upon leaning into the daily grind, holding your ground when you'd rather check out. Practicing presence calls for a certain openhandedness with God and where he is taking you. Practicing presence is looking plain old life square in the face and saying, *Yes, you're beautiful and you're mine. Let's do this.*

Like Mary, we all have choices to make; we all have the better thing to discover. Can you hear the whispers of what that might be? The hard parts you're skirting around? The struggle with complacency? Ask Jesus to sit with you a spell. Ask what he's doing behind the scenes, how he's building your life through your everyday moments. Ask him to meet you right in the middle of your discontentment and your daily work to encourage you to press on. To remind you that you're made in his image. To reassure you that your life has great meaning.

It won't be taken away from you.

seven

SWEAT, SPEEDOS, AND SPARKLY SURPRISES

'm somewhat of a hippie. Kind of granola, but not totally. If I were a bumper sticker, I'd land somewhere between "Kale yeah!" and "I love animals, they're delicious." I spent six years of my childhood on a mountain in Idaho without electricity or paved roads, and all the other years were spent on the beach in Southern California. So, while I love man-made things—especially my pink velvet couch with sequined cushions—I have a special affinity for creation, for experiencing God's presence in what he spoke into existence. I don't want to cram my earthy ways down your throat, as I understand not everyone enjoys the same things, but there is nothing quite as real and centering as delighting in nature.

And if nature is the doorway of God's wild beauty, then adventure is crossing the threshold with intention. It's not enough just to know it's there or to merely bring pieces of it into my house; it must be entered into. This call of adventure is an invitation to experience sights, sounds, scents, and textures that draw us out of ourselves and into what's happening beyond the sterile and controlled environments we have built around us.

I believe the pleasure of God is in the adventure—in the sound of fishing poles clacking while hiking down the trail, the picnic on the river, the casting and mending of the fly rod's thick white line under a wide blue sky; in the waxing of the board, the salt crystals forming on hair and eyelashes after surfing—yet we don't often recognize it. When we do, it's like opening an elegantly wrapped gift in the presence of the giver: there is mutual anticipation, mutual delight. He saw what he had made and called it *good*, and he wants us to revel in the good he made.

But, too often, we merely spend our days checking off the to-do list. He gave us senses he wants to fill, yet we've allowed them to be dulled by screens, by busyness, by duty. Sometimes the last thing on our minds is enjoying creation, looking for adventure. Maybe it's because work is relentless; the hamster wheel spins too fast to step down without face planting. Maybe it's because going off the beaten path takes a bit of effort, more than we think we can afford. Maybe it's because encountering nature can be an unpredictable thing, a bit frightening, because we might find ourselves in a situation we can't control. But I'm pretty sure that's where God meets us: in the space where we set aside our agenda and learn to be openhanded with his will for the days of our lives. He meets us in the wild and savage beauty because, as they say in Narnia, "He is not a tame lion."

So much keeps us from natural spaces—but isn't that where we met God for the first time, so long ago? In a garden. Face-to-face. Where it's his desire to care for us by filling our souls with fresh air, with exquisite beauty. It's his concept, that in creation we are drawn into his very presence. And in that presence, we are drawn closer to him and closer to each other. Being outside gives us the chance to stop to notice him, to hear him say, *Look what I made for you, my dear. Look how much I love you, how capable I am of creating beautiful things. Come away with me, darling. Be with me awhile.* It's hard to ignore when we step away from our usual distractions. Love is loud and clear in the great outdoors.

Entering into the adventure space is always a risk. Sometimes it ends up magical—the setting, the company, the weather, the discovery. And yet sometimes . . . not so much. You can't put a bridle on adventure; it's going to go the way it wants. Either way, though, it's *living*. It's diving into the experience. It's sharing in our surroundings and finding out more about ourselves, more about each other. And it's always beautiful, even if it looks a little different than we hoped.

✳

Let me confess something a teensy bit creepy: I like to sweat. I'm not talking about just hardcore workout sweat, although that is so satisfying, but I'm also talking everyday, run-of-the-mill, glistening-on-your-upper-lip sweat. The kind that rolls down your back like a tropical raindrop off a ginger leaf. Evidence of weather or evidence of physical exertion—it doesn't matter. I just like it. It's a manifestation of how God made our bodies with such ingenuity, and there's something so present about sweat—it means we felt the heat, that we entered into the burn of movement, adventure, play. Sweat means we didn't try to control our environment; it means we let it be what it was meant to be. It means we took a long walk on the beach with a friend on a hot day, or we danced uninhibited at a cousin's wedding. Sweat tells us what hemisphere of the planet we are on, what season it is. It is earthy and experiential; it is evidence of one's surroundings and activity. It's one of those physiological blessings of God, the built-in cooling system.

Britt, on the other hand, prefers never to release a single sweat droplet. He wants the AC forming icicles off his mustache. We have a long history of arguing in the car over the temperature. AC shooting out like Gru's freeze ray, forming ice blocks around my gladiator-sandaled feet, makes me cranky. When we ride in Britt's truck I need to plan ahead and bring a buffalo skin to survive the temporary blizzard. He does not enjoy the actual outside temperature, while I want the sunroof open and windows down.

We knew heading into the Holy Land was going to require something of a meteorological mediation between us. The temperatures in Israel during the fall are commonly above 100 degrees, so we were going right into an inferno. Oh, the marriage was about to be challenged.

In all our discussions beforehand, we had decided we wanted to approach this trip with intentional presence. We wanted to feel it all, taste it all, experience the whole thing fully. I decided I also wanted to feel the heat. Sweat would be one of the first tangible experiences of presence in Israel, manifest in the deep womb-like warmth of the sea, the sultry winds at sunset, the sun's reflection off ancient stone streets. We were foreigners living in a foreign land, and I didn't want to simply duplicate our American existence. Now, I'm not talking about never using the AC in the car or the apartment, but generally accepting the physical sensation of heat, of sweat, of the Israeli autumn that held our family in its embrace.

"We are living in Israel, man. This won't happen again. Let's feel it. Let's own it. Let's eat ice cream when it's hot. Let's swim and dry off in the sun. Let's eat our dinners on the apartment balcony. Let's invite the atmosphere in, not shut it out," I would say to Britt in the beginning. And other than shaking his head and saying, "You're so cosmic," there was no argument.

So, we drove with the windows down, in the open air, hearing the insults the Israeli drivers hurled at us (apparently, you must drive like a maniac to survive). We felt the hot wind through our fingertips on the highway to Jerusalem; we mopped sweat from our necks like ancient pilgrims. We were on an adventure, and part of our adventure of feeling it all and entering into the experience was exploration: this is where sweat and imagination and curiosity meet. Which may have killed the cat. At least it made the cat want to scratch her eyes out. You'll soon see where I'm going with this. Stay with me.

Whenever we weren't in the clinic, we were on a mission to hit up every awesome beach we could, and the more remote and mysterious, the better. The beaches in Tel Aviv and the surrounding areas were super crowded and chaotic. And it seemed like every Israeli male on the beach was constantly playing a game called Matkot, which is basically Smashball. But they didn't just play it; they destroyed it. All up and down the waterline, there were bronzed men in Speedos sending that little rubber ball flying so fast toward one another it could rupture a kidney from the front, should a player miss. Getting to the water for a swim was a life-or-death situation, explosions going off everywhere, little bombs whizzing from side to side, never stopping. And the noise. *Tock tock tock tock tock tock*, incessant and demanding. You'd think you'd gone mad. Covering the sand were groups of beachgoers, each with some sort of boom box competing in volume with their neighbors. American pop music over Israeli club music. Honestly, the noise level was such that it would be more peaceful to sunbathe at the airport.

And did I mention the cultural interpretation of personal space? Israelis sit so close to each other they can smell each other's breath. I don't know why. Perhaps they're making room to accommodate the entire country on the sand? It was so strange to us Americans, the way they wedged themselves up next to each other. Sardines all in a row. While tanning, we all practically had to flip to the other side simultaneously on the count of three. It was honestly too much to handle, this invasion of my personal space and assaulting of my senses.

Another thing that drove me crazy was the litter on the beaches. Apparently, no one's caught on to the whole reduce-reuse-recycle thing. Every time we would leave the beach I would pick up litter all the way to the parking lot and stuff it in the trash can. The locals would stare at me the entire time, puzzled by my actions. But I couldn't just leave it there, strewn all over the sand. It goes completely against my religion. I knew we had to find an alternative to the beach situation, lest this Cali girl go nuts.

Our search for nirvana commenced, and as we boycotted the crowded beaches for the rest of our time in Israel, it led to some pretty interesting discoveries. I had read that sea turtles frequented certain beaches in the vicinity and, during that time of year, were nesting on a particular secluded beach about forty-five minutes north of Tel Aviv. I couldn't wait to go there so that all my hippie/ homeschool/tree-hugging dreams could come true. I could just imagine our little family of four crouched down, witnessing the birth of a clutch of turtle babies. I could see their tiny yet wise-looking faces peeking through the fine white sand, blinking in the light. The sun would be on our backs, the wind gentle on our faces. And the sea would sparkle with the light of God.

It turned out there would be some sparkle, all right. But let's not get ahead of ourselves. After a fair bit of wrong turns, dirt roads through various veggie crops, and dead ends, we found the trailhead that would take us to this magical beach. There were a few cars parked there to my dismay, because I really was hoping to have it all to ourselves. *Shake it off and just enjoy*, I said to myself. *Perfection won't be until heaven, so just accept the day and the adventure for what it is*. I was determined that the day would be perfect, even if I had to share it with a few strangers.

We unloaded the kids from our puny little car, along with grocery-store boogie boards, a picnic lunch, beach blankets, books, basically all the things we needed for our pilgrimage. And a pilgrimage it became. We started hiking the trail, a knot of twists and turns, not know-ing where exactly we were supposed to go. The sun beat down, and I felt like Sarah following Abraham to an unknown land, laden with provisions, sweat pouring in the heat of the high sun. We walked and walked. Daisy needed to be carried on Britt's back, and Isaiah asked me 432 times when we would get to the beach. I started to wonder where we were going and if we would make it. I prepared to die on the sandy cliffs above the beach, vultures plucking out my eyeballs. *They were so close*, the mourners would say. *Their adventuresome spirit was admirable. They will be greatly missed. Rest in peace, fearless globetrotters.*

After a good half hour (it honestly felt like half a lifetime), we made it to a steep but passable trail on the cliff down to the beach. And the beach was glorious! A long stretch, white sand crisp next to the deep turquoise of the Mediterranean in the fall. Sheer glory, pure beauty, all to ourselves. Well, almost.

As we started down the treacherous path with dirt and pebbles rolling down over our feet and scattering down the hill, I came across a man. He looked at me, then looked at the rest of my family. I couldn't quite decipher the look on his face, but it registered closely as confusion. We were obviously not local, and perhaps he wondered how these brave travelers were so lucky as to unlock the secrets of nature in the Holy Land. I guessed he was thinking, *Look at those daring Westerners. Their kids are so blessed to have such adventurous parents.* Yes, I'm sure that's what he was thinking.

We made it safely down to the bottom of the cliff just as another man was about to climb up. He also gave us a look we couldn't decipher, but who cares? This beach was gloriously uninhabited! We threw our burdens down in a heap, sundresses and tee shirts flying, and ran straight for the water. The fresh air, the salty sea, the privacy from the cliffs all felt a bit like a dream come true. Some nature in a world that had become concrete, some open space in a life that had become crowded. Quiet, peace, beauty, all for us, all for my little family. I came out of the water, hair dripping, and lay down on my towel. The hot sun left little salt crystals on my eyelashes as it evaporated the water, and in my reverie and calm, cheek resting on my folded arms, I gazed at our personal paradise through eyes half-closed like a lazy cat in a patch of sunlight.

The dreamlike feel of the day took a sharp turn when, through my sleepy, contented haze, I noticed a person down the beach. My beach. My personal private beach. That was a little irritating, but it got worse. It wasn't what the person had on that I noticed, but what the person did not have on. There was a naked man sauntering peacock-proud down the beach after a swim, the water sparkling on his skin from head to toe. The beach we had discovered was uncrowded and off the beaten path because it was, in fact, a nude beach. Yes, I had taken my family to a nude beach in a foreign land.

Suddenly I noticed the sparkling naked man wasn't the only one; there were more even farther down. I sat bolt upright as I felt panic rise up in me, the realization dawning of what we had plopped ourselves in the middle of. *Dear God, please don't let me see that man up close. Please don't let my kids see him up close. If you get us off this beach unscathed, I promise anything you want. I'll give you all my money. I'll give you all my time. Just rescue us from the . . .*

"Mommy! Why is that man all sparkly? Mommy, is

that man naked?" Daisy's sweet voice jolted me out of my prayerful plea.

"Oh, um, I don't know. Maybe his shorts are tan? Um, I think we should go now, guys. I'm pretty sure it's time for ice cream!" my strained reply came forth, while I threw on my clothes and called the boys out of the water. "Babe!" I yelled, my previous leisurely tone and tenor completely gone. "Babe! Let's go!" I said, a forced smile on my face as I tried my best to keep it cool, praying the kids didn't notice our fellow beachgoers' au naturel frolic.

We found ourselves scampering back up the steep cliff we had come down so careful and expectant, having seen no turtles but bringing home a good laugh. The beachgoers? Well, I'm sure they had a good laugh too. So much for our adventure. But it was what it was supposed to be, I think. We had entered into it—the searching, the hiking, the discovery, the shared mortification. We were there; we felt the salt water wash off the dirt and sweat. We were all in, together. And though it wasn't quite what we had hoped, it was a gift that brought us closer together. Days like that are precious: Learning together, laughing. The lack of controlled environment, letting it be what it was.

❋

I love the freedom of wilderness, of adventure. I always have, but the years of first learning to be a mother, and then the years of hospitals, protocols, and sterilized medical appointments had beaten that love right out of me. The paramount responsibility for another little life had convinced me to set the love of adventure aside dutifully, giving me the illusion of control as I was careful about every little thing. But that illusion had sucked the joy out of the present. Careful! Yield! Danger! No loitering! No swimming! No loud noises! Designated spaces, restrictive signs, all the things we set in place to make our minds up for us and tell us what to do, rip us off from the real life that's happening right before us. If we had stayed on the beaten path those months we spent in Israel, if we had continued to obey the signs, to cram in like sardines and go the way everyone else was going, we only would have experienced dirty, crowded beaches. We never would have found that glorious, gorgeous seaside sanctuary. And we never would have had the shared—if mortifying—memory that makes us laugh every time we think of it now.

I think in order to feel that permission to explore, to set aside our anxiety and circumstances and just be, there's a certain amount of trust required. Perhaps that's the best part of it all, trusting God. Just like it takes trust to obey him within the boundaries he has set in his Word—like with our money, our relationships, our sexuality—it takes trust to let go of unnecessary constraints and freely enjoy the gift of life. To give up manipulation and enter into what your life actually is currently, not what you wish it was. It all takes trust. And the way trust works with the beautiful freedom God gives makes for a life well lived. It takes trust to enter into delight, into adventure. It takes trust to accept the gift of creation and make time for exploration of nature. It takes trust when things don't go as planned, and it takes trust to know that what God is doing will be beautiful, on and off the beach.

Even now, after all our adventures overseas, after the rise and fall of hope during Daisy's sickness, after the spark of new life in the aftermath of loss, the daily grind of motherhood and work and home-keeping, I have to remind myself that it's good and right to spend time playing. I have to trust God with the joy of adventure, because it's not my go-to anymore. I have to expect good things from him, listening for him in creation. I have to remember that he takes pleasure when I do.

We don't live in a perfect world, but we do live in a beautiful one, and I don't want our plastic tendencies to overshadow what's authentic, what's divine. I don't want to miss the chance to play in the garden, to meet God in the cool of the day. I want to get off the hamster wheel and invest in the rhythms of creation, I want to make space to explore; it paves the way to nearness with him. It will be messy, maybe stinky sometimes. It will be organic and unpredictable and require commitment. But it will be beautiful, good, healing. It's part of searching for real. In earth and sky and gardening and surfing, in trees and prayer and laughter and sun, I see him, and we are together.

Not all of us live near a white sand beach; not all of us live in alpine glory. But I'm guessing there might be a vegetable garden nearby or an arboretum. Or maybe for you adventure is laying a blanket out on your lawn and letting the sunshine and your babies crawl all over you. Maybe it means saying yes to a trip to the desert with girlfriends, watching the stars unveil themselves one by one. Maybe it means building a snowman with your niece. Perhaps it's a meandering walk in your own neighborhood, praying and breathing in wildflowers alongside the road, sun shining full on your face. Whatever that looks like, you know what's calling out to you. I know you hear it, feel the twitch of excitement when you think of somewhere you'd like to visit. Make it happen, my friend. Whether that means loading up the van with elementary schoolers and inner tubes to go to the river or hopping a plane to Tuscany, God is waiting for you there.

eight

THESE THINGS ARE FIREPROOF

S nuggled down deep in borrowed covers, I stared out the window, unable to sleep. It was three thirty in the morning, and Fifi tossed next to me, loudly sucking her thumb, straddling that place between clinging to wakefulness and letting go into dreamland. The sky was lit up orange, smoke and ashes falling like snow. *It is December, after all*, I thought with an inner chuckle. As I stared, I fell in and out of sleep. I thought. And I dreamed. But my dreams soon turned to flames, to lost treasures, to blackened hope.

It started like so many things do, with the fire being someone else's problem. I had awoken a week ago to a massive plume of orange and gray in the sky, hovering over Ventura, about eighteen miles from my home. Shaking my head in pity and saying prayers for the afflicted, I silently thanked God it wasn't my problem. There was no way it would follow its fiery path this far. And anyhow, wildfires are common here in California. So common, in fact, I recently told my friend from Texas, with a toss of the hand, "Oh sure, they happen all the time! It's totally no big deal." Isn't that how it always is? Disasters and misfortunes only happen to other people. Until they happen to us.

It's funny, I've always wondered what I would take with me in case of evacuation. In fact, last week, while I was still smug and sure the fire wouldn't reach us, I'd had a conversation with Britt about what we would pack if our house were ever on fire. This was my list: my computer (I'm halfway through the manuscript at this point, and losing it would mean losing my cool, present, contented vibe), photo albums with Daisy in them, journals and little papers she had written on, and my retainers. Because I sneeze and my teeth move, and I'm not about to evacuate, lose my house, *and* get braces for the fourth time.

But then my silent, self-satisfied prayer of thanks turned into an evacuation notice two days later, which sent me wandering around my house deciding what was worth packing up and what could be left behind to burn. When the fires were still far away and my friends in Ventura were evacuating, I had mentally pared my existence down to about one duffel bag. But when it was my turn, it wasn't quite that simple. I wandered through the rooms, at a loss for what to pack. Which jeans fit best? How many pairs of underwear? Will I want my Birkenstocks? Britt hates them, but they're so comfy and totally on trend. It's a shame to leave that Free People dress behind; you just don't find embroidery like that every day. How about my new gray sweater dress with the cute puffy sleeves? *Stop being vain, Kate. All this can be replaced. Go for the sentimental, the heirlooms, the spiritual, and some practical.* So, I decided on several pairs of underwear, one pair of jeans, extra PJs, and, indeed, the list I had casually mentioned to my husband. I packed the little lion made of rope that my grandfather bought for my grandmother at a Paris flea market when he was in the Royal Air Force. I packed random framed pictures, a few favorite books, my riding boots, and the first Bible Britt ever bought me. It was hardly enough. It was almost too much.

There is just no way to look at your life through the lens of possessions, of mere things, and have a full understanding of leaving it behind, of what it all means. The meaning of home. The meaning of your family history and personal style, of kids' artwork and surfboards and pet chickens. Of years of study and learning and toys left behind by Daisy who left before us. The meaning of comfort, of wardrobe and linens, of children's books and old Frye boots. The items that surround my habits of being on a daily basis, the familiar textures and dishes and the silver bowl engraved "Sylvia and Max," my grandparents' nicknames for each other. How do you add it all up? How do you place value on one thing above another? It's times like this that stare us in the face, that cause us to take stock of where our values lie. It's times like this that burn the dross off our tangible, everyday lives and give us reason to think about our priorities. It's times like this we are offered a chance to practice presence while the crutch of worldly goods and stability crumbles beneath us.

I ended up with one duffel bag of things and decided the rest would be either all or nothing. So, nothing it is.

As I write this, it has been five nights of evacuation. I took the kids up to San Luis Obispo to stay with friends and get out of the smoke. We had a great time, with only one poop emergency and one barf episode. Neither one involved my kid, but the poop emergency was on my watch. And since it takes a village, I was inclined to conquer the situation. My own children sufficiently contributed to the excitement with a split-open chin in the lobby of a swanky hotel (Fifi), along with a near-brawl on the beach with a cranky local (Isaiah). We dubbed our time there "evacu-cation."

It was almost glamorous to evacuate, to appear blasé about the whole thing. *I'm so cool about it, you know. It's just stuff, no big. Let's just all be present.* Except being evacuated is secretly stressful—what with driving around with all your most prized possessions in the back of the car, finding things to do that satisfy both a three-year-old and a seventeen-year-old, not sleeping much, and realizing I only brought one pair of pants. Plus, I was just wishing I was in my own home.

Since the fires seemed to not come too close to my neighborhood and we appeared to be in the clear, I decided I would just hit up Home Depot, grab a box of masks, and saunter home in all my contented glory. I drove back home from San Luis Obispo to be with Britt and hopefully get some rest. He had stayed behind with the firefighters to defend our ranch, and for four days had been riding his dirt bike all over the canyon watching for ember fires, soaking our property with hoses and sprinklers, and preparing for the approaching flames. I pulled into the driveway, let him take care of Fifi, and went straight to bed for a nap. That evening was one of those ethereal, peaceful, calm-before-the-storm times. Britt barbecued elk steaks and made a lemony-garlicky salad while I took a bath with essential oils and watched the sky glow red through the misty bathroom window. I've never had a more elegant afternoon.

We went to bed around 9:30 p.m. only to wake up at 11:40 to a phone call. The fire was closing in, they said, stay alert. By 1:40 a.m. the entire beautiful, magical hillside was aflame, having blazed past the firebreak the firemen had built. It devoured the brush and trees, ravenous like a kid who'd spent the whole day swimming. Britt ran outside into the ashy night for a few minutes and came back in, telling me to stay calm and to get Fifi in the car.

"Don't stop," he said, eyes burning into mine. "Go straight to my parents' house."

Outside, with Fifi in my arms and the canyon engulfed in flames, the glow was unearthly and the anticipation electric. But deeper, more radical and moving, was the roar, the sound of the consuming of fuel, of relentless devastation bigger than any human can contain. The fire was coming, and it was coming quick.

Isaiah hopped into his beat-up little truck and followed after me as we drove through the canyon I love so much. We drove past fire trucks, past men in the yellow fireproof suits, baggy around the boots. We drove past hoses and caution tape and all the human effort we could muster, yet it was unstoppable. I could see smaller fires spontaneously igniting a mile away from the main wildfire, threatening homes, avocado ranches, a boarding school, and farms. Ironically, we flew past Smokey the Bear in silence, tall and proud with his furry round belly and ranger hat, his sign letting us know that today's fire risk was extreme while the ashes piled up on it like snow. The mountain half of my agricultural seaside town was ablaze, and I was hurtling through with my little girl in the back seat, ashes floating gently down and scampering off the windshield.

When we arrived at our destination, we knocked and were let in by loving and comforting arms. I acted breezy about the whole thing, determined to keep Fifi excited about the adventure rather than feeding off my apprehension. We scratched the dogs, we hugged the grandparents, and then we settled in while the fire wreaked the greatest devastation our town has known. I cuddled my little girl in the guest room bed. We whispered stories and secrets and made plans to go out for ice cream. But as she drifted off, I lay there. I lay there and shivered, just a little bit, and wondered if my house still stood. The house that held Daisy's artwork, my grandmother's silver, my son's journals and drawings. The house that was the last earthly place Daisy drew breath.

It's all just stuff, I told myself. *Yes, just stuff.*

But some of that stuff held my heart.

※

The question of what matters most hits right between the eyes when we are confronted with the possibility of loss, when we are told to choose what's most important and make darn sure it fits in the back of the Toyota. There is stuff we need, yes, like the things I chose to pack up, but the rest of it is optional, merely an enhancement to life. It is exactly in these situations of potential loss, when we are evaluating what is essential and what is optional, that we need to take an honest look at where we are in terms of contentment. Have we, like the apostle Paul, learned the secret of contentment? Or have we let our routines and possessions and busyness usurp the things of true value?

It's Christmastime, and part of the stillness, the strangeness of this year, is that there is so much that is not happening because of the fires. Classes aren't being held; Christmas programs are canceled. Parties are postponed, and the last thing I want to do is build a fire in the fireplace. We have been ushered into each other's presence, into openhanded contentment and simplicity, by force. It's almost like all the nonessential parts of life have been burned away, and what's left is what is real. Family, mealtimes, waiting out the fire and smoke together until we can all get on with our lives. But isn't that what life actually is in the first place? It's as if all the extras, the optional things and distractions, were lifted to gift us time with family and meals shared and slow days. Being in crisis sheds light, does it not? So, we play cards and do another puzzle. We escape the smoke for a day in Malibu; we huddle together with grateful hearts.

The danger is past now, but my neighborhood is still under mandatory evacuation. Luckily, we know a path through avocado orchards and over a hill to get around the police barricades and to our house. We've been here a couple of nights already, and while it's eerie to live in this canyon while every other property is evacuated, we don't want to be anywhere but home. I am keenly aware that not everyone has a home to come back to, that though we are war-torn we are the lucky ones this time. Outside my kitchen window I see black and gray; the hills are a moonscape. There is silence. A severe stillness. It's the end of a long exhale, as I survey the land around me. The calm before the storm is a real thing, yes, but the smolder after the fire is another. The canyon groans with the scorching; the entire scene reeks of apocalyptic ruin. But my affection for it runs as deep as ever.

The creatures have scattered; the wildflowers are gone. The trees that remain appear a desiccated shadow of themselves. It will be a while until the devastation rights itself. It will be a while until I can bask in the deep pink light reflected off the chaparral that grows up the side of the hill. Even so, those are my mountains, my view, and not a day goes by that I don't look at them and cherish the fact that my house borders the wild. And yet the wild is exactly that. Unpredictable.

It's not the things we fill our homes with or the packed schedules we keep or our mass of followers or sense of control that gives us peace. No, it's the wild, deep-rooted, rich things in life that bring true contentment. The community, the land. The work, the play. The prayer, the intercession. The face-to-face conversations, the child in our arms. The outpour to one another, the love through service. It's the openhearted inclination toward what life brings us today and the presence of who we share it with. And as far as the evacuation packing list goes, it's the memories attached to the things, not the things themselves. You can't burn these things to ashes; these things are fireproof.

Standing at the sink, two days after the fire has passed, I stare out at those bald mountains as I cover a pot of dried black beans with water to soak. I see the splotches of white ash, the crooked black outlines of singed trees, and I am hyperaware of my blessings. I am safe inside my home. There is once again a mess on my floor, and there is chicken in my slow cooker. My daughter is napping; my son is surfing. My husband just called from work to see if he should romp his truck over the mountain or merely outrun the police to get home past the evacuation barriers. These moments make up my life: the harrowing, the peaceful, the dangerous, and the dreary. The coming to terms with possessions, with routines, with contentment and security. And I smile to myself, because I realize that despite the ashes, life, in all its wild unpredictability, is beautiful.

nine

CAN I GET A WITH-NESS?

Tel Aviv is a tangle of concrete, buildings, cars, exhaust, and armed guards. At first, we were swept up in the metropolis, gasping for air. We definitely felt like outsiders, unwieldy and unwelcome, trying to find a place to fit in. After a few hits and misses, we finally found a respite to turn to and ended up spending countless lunchtimes at a corner café called Streets. It was a hip little joint on the corner of a busy street, with black metal chairs, black-and-white photos on the walls, and a cement trough sink in between the men's and women's bathrooms—so progressive. The kids working there were all so beautiful in their own way. The girl with half her head shaved and huge glasses. The boy with the curly black afro and striped tee shirts. The high-waisted pants, the looping hem of the fluorescent tank tops, the worn high-top sneakers. They wore piercings and jewelry anywhere they pleased with hair cut angular and asymmetrical. The hip uniform of the young and the free, of the kids who had shrugged off the religion of their parents. They looked like they were from my hometown, and they captured our hearts.

The café was a few blocks down from the clinic, so it became our go-to before or after treatment. Daisy and

Isaiah usually opted for the schnitzel, while Britt and I noshed on salads and pizza. We would sit, the four of us, in our same spot on the patio. Britt a head taller than most of the population, tan and blond. I was fifteen inches shorter than him, also sporting the fresh-off-the-beach look (which secretly means I don't brush my hair and totally get away with it). Isaiah was the coolest little blondie wearing black Ray-Bans with prescription lenses, and Daisy sparkled with her magnetic personality, freckles, and bald head. Needless to say, we stuck out a bit among the Israeli hipsters.

From the first day we walked into that café, the servers were friendly to us. We would sit for a couple of hours sometimes, killing time before treatment. We played cards over and over, our bottoms planted on those trendy black chairs. And, without fail, those darling young Israelis would show us kindness, usually in the form of a treat on the house. Sometimes it was a huge and luscious wedge of cold watermelon garnished with mint and feta; other times it was a perfectly round scoop of icy pink gelato. Once it was tall skinny glasses of lemonade slush, particularly refreshing in the sultry weather.

We came to love those kids, love the way they treated us. We learned their names and shared hugs, and they loved us too. They had become a sweet connection to the land, to the people. One day, as the boy with the afro brought over yet another gift for us to eat, my husband looked up at him and said, "Why are you so nice to us?"

Embarrassed, he looked away and, in a voice barely intelligible, said, "It is our mitzvot." *Mitzvot*, the plural of *mitzvah*, is a commandment from God. God commanded his people to perform acts of kindness—a tangible way to give and receive his love. The boy with the afro and his coworkers saw a dying girl and her family and poured out love the best way they knew how.

This was a stunning revelation. The kindness, the love, the intentional connection with what's right in front of us—all this was God's idea. It came back to him. He was behind the comforting gestures, the feeling of fitting in and simply being *with* each other. He is behind all of our deep longings for relationship, and he personified it when his Son walked the earth.

❊

Mary of Bethany has haunted my thoughts for a while now. I imagine her in that ancient, dusty, delightful place. Her story shows me that something really precious lies beneath our need for being people of presence. Something more than unplugging, more than putting overconnection and overcommitment in its place. Something more than just rising above our current circumstances, more than just enjoying a physically and emotionally healthy way of being. There's a profoundly sacred reason we are driven to discover what's most important.

I've been going on and on about presence, about choosing peace and contentment. I've talked about being with—truly *with*—each other, about living intentionally and openly. These are healthy things, yes. They are beneficial and wise and fruitful things. But beyond that, there is a fundamentally better reason for shifting our hearts to practice these things, one that I believe Mary saw as she sat at Jesus' feet with all the chaos swirling around her. One that caused her to make a cameo in another story that made history, as told in the book of John.

Let's enter Bethany again. Another dinner party, more time with Jesus, more of Martha's bustling about. Another dinner in Jesus' honor, another time of human connection, of sharing food and space and trust. Another evening when God Made Flesh came into a little house in a little town and broke bread with a little group of friends. And by this point, as his short and powerful ministry was winding down and he was making his way to Jerusalem to perform the most loving act in history, this Emmanuel had shown himself to be healer, teacher, and lifter of unruly heads. This Miracle Maker had walked on water, healed the sick, given sight to the blind, and offered living water. He had shown Israel who he really was—by his words, his deeds, his presence. Redeemer. Bread of Life. Prince of Peace. Lamb of God. And he was right there. With them. With the stress case (Martha). With the activist (Simon). With the traitor (Judas). With the formerly dead (Lazarus). With the avaricious (Matthew) and the country boys (Philip, Bartholomew, Andrew) and the rabble-rousers (James and John). With the garrulous (Peter). With the doubter (Thomas). With all these raga-muffins he loved so much.

And Mary. Doe-eyed, present, peaceful Mary. Mary, who had discovered the better thing, the thing most worth being concerned about. Who made room for with-ness, who experienced the peace and joy that with-ness sustains. Mary gracefully entered the scene, among all the bubbling conversations, debates, and personalities, among the various scents and tapestries and clay pitchers and wooden bowls. Quietly, she slipped into the room, maybe catching her brother Lazarus's eye, maybe taking a deep breath. She carried with her an alabaster jar of perfume, one that cost an entire year's wages. All of her wealth, all of her trust, all of her future she carefully held in that thin, fragile, ethereally elegant vessel. I can see it now, the careful steps she takes, tiptoeing into the room bursting with masculine voices and smelling like spicy food and men sweaty and dusty from the journey. The whole room, swirling with distraction, thick with cultural expectation and tradition. She kept her eyes on Jesus, regardless of the trepidation she must have felt, knowing her actions might again be criticized.

And yet.

The draw of Jesus was so cogent that, right there, in the middle of all the distractions, in front of all the befuddled dinner guests, Mary moved toward Jesus as if it were just the two of them in the room. There, she gave all she had. She broke the jar, poured it out over Jesus' feet, and, using her hair as a towel, she lovingly covered him in her most precious possession. She was with him, in the distraction, in the wake of miracles, in the face of his impending death. She was with him, in love and adoration, knowing he would be gone soon. And her worship and with-ness filled the whole house with an intense fragrance. Mary had learned what was most important, all right. What had started with giving Jesus her full attention, choosing to listen in the face of distraction, had culminated in an act of worship that went down in history. Worship flowed from their intimacy, from their with-ness. Talk about relationship goals.

*

The profundity of God's presence has a ripple effect. Mary's example teaches me that presence breeds contentment, intimacy, trust, beauty, and joy, that it's fragrant and lasting. It teaches me that when we sit in God's presence, all these things will be in the flow, both to us and from us. That the peace I chase after, the love I long for, the acceptance and direction and courage I seek will be found in with-ness. Isn't that what most satisfies? Isn't it true love that we are chasing after with all our overcommitted madness, our social media addiction, our frenzy to succeed and belong and achieve?

Jesus still offers this same profound presence; he has sat down and is waiting to see if we'll sit with him. I see this invitation to with-ness in Mary's story; I see it in his disciples' stories. I see it woven throughout the stories of his life on earth. And I can see myself in the people he met with: the woman with the issue of blood, outcast and lonely; the child without social status, unseen and unvalued; the blind beggar, depressed and destitute; the woman at the well, sinful and broken. It's that spark of attention, the offering of himself, that moment in the crowd when he says, "I see you." It's pure love.

Are you seeing a pattern? The one that threads the whole of human history, all the lengths God has gone to just to be *with* us? Let your mind wander back over the love letter we call the Bible. From the beginning in the garden, to the years of prophecy and animal sacrifice, to the appearance and sacrifice of Jesus, God has made a way to be with us and for us to be with him. But not just in heaven; I'm talking *right now.*

Let these verses blow your mind:

Psalm 116:1–2 tells us, "I love the LORD because he hears my voice and my prayer for mercy. *Because he bends down to listen,* I will pray as long as I have breath!"

Psalm 139:17–18 proclaims, "How precious are your thoughts about me, O God. They cannot be numbered! I can't even count them; they outnumber the grains of sand! And when I wake up, you are still *with me!*"

Zephaniah 3:17 declares, "For *the LORD your God is*

living among you. . . . He will rejoice over you with joyful songs."

Jesus told his disciples as he ascended to heaven in Matthew 28:20, "And be sure of this: *I am with you always,* even to the end of the age" (my emphasis on all these verses).

Are you hearing what I'm hearing? The Creator of the Universe wants to be *with* me; he wants to be with you! Can you just see him bending down to listen? Gentle and slow, just the two of you in the world. Can you feel the warmth of his breath on you, sweet and comforting? Can you feel your face in his hands, see his eyes fixed on yours and full of love? Picture that with me. Let's sit in that a moment and let it stir our hearts and remind us we are adored children; let it bring out all the wonder and hope we've been missing.

He sees us. He loves us. He hears us. And he wants to be *with us.*

This has been the salient point in my journey to presence and all across the Holy Land. With-ness reflects the nature of God, just like Jesus. All the stories I've told, all the experiences we've had, were filled with good and true and beautiful things, yet were not the point themselves. All the habits I learned that promote presence, all the small choices, all the focus and quiet and taking stock of what's important—all these things had a foundation, an impetus. If God bends down to listen to me, then that's what I want to do with my people. If Jesus made time to be alone with his Father, then so will I. If the very gospel is about with-ness, the best love story ever to come true, then that's what I want my life to echo.

Let me tell you something I've learned the hard way: God is willing to speak to and lead us more than we are willing to be spoken to and led. God feels far sometimes, but he hasn't gone anywhere. Isaiah 30:18 tells us that he is waiting for us just so he can have compassion on us. Both in the Psalms and from Jesus we are told to cast our burdens on him. That's the beauty of prayer: the simple act of stopping, of offering Jesus our presence. Prayer is the beginning of presence, the beginning of peace, the beginning of contentment.

That simple act is easier said than done, though. I am all too human, and I confess that if I wait until the end of the day to pray, I barely give Jesus more than a minute as my head hits the pillow before it's lights out, and even then I go straight to what I want from him. Like, *Hey, Jesus, will you please* . . . and the snoring ensues. Can you imagine if that was all the attention my man gave me? Yeah, that would be a problem. Especially if he gave me just enough to ask me to do stuff for him, then checked out. *Hey, babe, do my laundry . . . snore.*

But all foibles of humanity aside, I am acutely aware of the relational effects of communication. Because we are always communicating something to one another, aren't we? Even in our lack of it. If the only communication happening under my roof is perfunctory or obligatory, the people who live here will begin to believe we don't love each other. And if the only communicating that happens between me and God is perfunctory or obligatory, I will begin to believe he doesn't love me. When loving and intimate communication doesn't happen, the accuser is the one communicating—and I hate what he has to say.

I've found this to be the case recently. Just last month, I picked up my journal, blew off the dust, and decided to just sit with God and see what happened. It had been so long. Not knowing where to start, I used a devotional guide with prayer prompts. In response to the selected portion of Scripture, one of the prompts asked me to make a list of the things God loves about me. I sat in the quiet, searching my soul, listening hard. Crickets. I started to feel uncomfortable with the silence, uncomfortable with the prompt. I wanted to toss the stupid book, get it out of my face. Defeated, I realized that the only thing I could come up with was not a list of the things God loves about me, but rather a list of things to fix. I was out of the practice of constant communication with him, and I couldn't fathom hearing things like grace or affection. Good stuff like that was for other people, not for me. But it turns out I had been too often listening to the accuser. I was listening to the voice of death, not the Author of Life.

When I dug in and spent the time, when I opened my ears and my heart, not only did I find out that I'm not a list of things to fix, but rather, I'm made in his image. I found out that God sings over me. That he has compassion for me, that he thinks of me and loves me. When I listen to the accusations and lies of the enemy rather than the words of love and affirmation from God, there is only chaos. But if I'm in union with God, then I'm walking in perfect peace. The union is in the communication. I talk; he listens. He talks; I listen. Just the two of us, intentionally listening, intentionally receiving.

It's the intentionality that's the problem, though. I'm pretty intentional when it comes to my flesh. I intentionally eat delicious food, intentionally make myself comfortable. But I need to remember that I am a whole being, and just like it's good to care for my flesh, it's important to care for my spirit. I need both. Just like Mary did as she sat raptly listening to Jesus. Even though there were guests all around and there was work to be done, she saw her opportunity and took it. She sat intentionally drinking in his words, devouring the Bread of Life. Showing up is intentionality. Sitting in silence is too. That's where we posture ourselves to listen with a willingness to respond.

For years, my prayers sounded a lot like a monologue. *Hey, God, here's my list of needs and some of my wants. Thanks, gotta go!* But lately prayer is more of a dialogue, one that takes turns and goes deeper, one filled with laughing and weeping, maybe even a bit of questioning or complaining. It's praying through the Scriptures, allowing God to speak, and giving myself the space to respond. And it's journaling. I used to hate journaling! But I discovered this whole new level of presence that it affords, how it anchors my thoughts. When I sit in stillness writing my prayer, my thoughts make more sense, my mind drifts less, and I can better hear the Lord speaking to me. It's quality time with Jesus. And when I remember that he is waiting for me, that he wants to be with me, I feel loved, comforted, cared for, encouraged.

❋

Sitting with God in communion, hearing him and being heard, is where we begin our practice of presence—and then we let that practice spill over into all facets of our lives, creating life-giving habits of being. And so we practice presence first by intentionally making space to open our hearts up to God, whether it's a comfy chair by a window watching the sunrise, while scrubbing floors, or on the morning subway commute bolting through the underground. We pray. We journal. We pore over the Scriptures.

And then we practice presence by eliminating distractions that close us off from God. Our phones, screens, the tyranny of the urgent. Did you know that Susanna Wesley (mother of the great preacher John Wesley) had so many children, the only thing she could do to get alone with God was pull her apron over her head? Each season has its own challenges, so we rise to the occasion.

And we practice presence by agreeing with what God is already saying to us. By asking him to take us further into our current season, accepting direction, receiving strength for hard days, or getting permission to fully enjoy today.

We practice presence by asking him to show us just how near he really is, how he sees us, and believing what he says rather than our own feelings, impressions, or emotions.

We practice presence by making space for recreation and rest, by going deeper into the mystery of creation and the gift of Sabbath. By stopping to see his hand on this world and trusting him to take the wheel once in a while.

We practice presence by moving from our comfort zones and into sharing ourselves with our community. By knowing others around us and making ourselves known, understanding that we are designed to need each other.

We practice presence by choosing whose voice we listen to, starting first thing in the morning. By choosing to listen to the voice of truth, beauty, and goodness, rather than starting our day by checking Facebook.

We practice presence by engaging in God's purposes around us. What is he doing in your community, in your family, in your heart? How can we be like Mary and choose to plop down in front of Jesus in the middle of the action and be a part of it? Whether it's loving your people, championing justice, or serving behind the scenes?

And we practice presence, just like Jesus was the reflection of the Father, by reflecting his glory as image bearers, not only his creativity in our art and work and daily living, but his relationality. If he bends down to listen to us, so shall we to our people. If his desire is to dwell among us, so should we desire to live in community. And if he is promising to be with us always, let us take him up on the offer. It's simple and beautiful *with-ness*.

Unwrapping the gift of presence has been a learning process. More than just a healthy way of being, I'm learning that the practice of presence is spiritually necessary. That it's not only healing and peaceful but it reflects God's image. That it's God-ordained; it's experiencing with-ness in a whole new way. It reminds me that there is a higher reason to give my people my full attention, because God has given me his. The wholeness of creation, the mystery of prayer, and the grandest love story ever known are rooted in the God who is with us. Emmanuel.

ten

KICKING BUTT AND
TAKING NAMES

Writing a book is like chiseling something recognizable out of a shapeless slab of stone. After doing a good bit of meticulous close-up work, you need to take a step back and look at the whole, scanning and searching for rough parts to smooth over, to edit. Editing in general is a most wonderful and necessary tool if you want to achieve any sort of style, function, or comprehension in a body of writing. And by editing, I mean cutting out what's unnecessary, what detracts from the main thing, what's dead weight. Pruning plants is a form of editing: trimming off the old parts so that new growth can thrive. You can also edit your wardrobe, tossing what is ill fitting, outdated, or in disrepair so that you have a better chance of leaving the house without looking color-blind or disillusioned (how arduous a task it is to part with the pants that once zipped up like butter but now can't get past the bod that made butter her best friend).

Editing a book is perhaps the most important part of the whole writing process. An editor takes a lump of words that in many parts looks a bit like a Picasso painting and makes it look more like da Vinci, putting the eyes, nose, and mouth where they belong. It makes for a smoother, more comprehensive read. Jessica, my editor, is fabulous at her job. She is brilliant, sharp, mindful, has the ability to see the big picture, and is especially kind and tactful when something is amiss. Let me illustrate her absolute importance in my life.

When I was writing my first book, *And Still She Laughs*, we had a good thing going. Though I cringed pretty hard when I received my manuscript back covered in redline—looking like it got into a catfight in a rainstorm—I eventually found out that was par for the course. We used Word, and along with making edits, we could write notes to each other in the margins, explaining our reasoning for a deletion or asking each other about preference in wording. Now, because I am a Christian woman writing with a Christian publisher, I realize there are a few turns of phrase that are perhaps better suited in a different outlet. I may or may not have included such a word in my first manuscript. Okay, so the word I am referring to rhymes with "happy" and starts with "cr." Jessica gently informed me that some book distributors would frown on that, and unless it was the hill I wanted to die on, I needed to pick a different word. Honestly, as a first-time author I couldn't afford to get under anyone's skin just yet, so I reverently changed the word to "rotten." There. Fixed.

Now, I wouldn't describe myself as a naturally self-aware person, so in all my correspondence with my editor, I worked hard to be vigilant in my word choices. We had established a relationship during editing, and I had a habit of writing little funny things in the margin, hoping to make her job a bit more entertaining. When we got to chapter 7, which was about feeling confident and powerful in the face of fear, I decided that my use of the phrase "kicking butt and taking names" should perhaps have a note to her in the margin, particularly after the previous snafu.

"Hey, is it okay to use this phrase? Or will someone get their knickers in a knot?" I asked Jessica, proud of myself for covering my bases and not giving her another need to tactfully tell me that won't fly. I decided I needed to explain further, though, in case she was feeling iffy.

"It's just that my husband coined the phrase, and I think it's absolutely hilarious."

Okay, if you're reading that right now and wondering what on earth I'm talking about, prepare to put the book down and walk away. You might have thought I was a reasonably educated woman, having written two books and all, but it turns out I am a bona fide blond in every sense of the word. I actually thought Britt made that phrase up because he used to say it all the time. In fact, I remember one day lounging on the bed and chatting with him while he was getting dressed for work. I, stay-at-home mom with a baby attached to my hip at all times, mentioned how impressed I was with all the stuff he had to do that day. He turned around to look at me while pulling his shirt over his head and said with gusto, "I'm kickin' butt and takin' names!"

It just struck me as funny, and as I fell all over myself laughing, he winked at me and said, "I made that up." Sigh, young love.

Now, I was completely unaware he was joking, and since I hadn't heard anyone else use that phrase, I took him at face value. Unfortunately, I didn't find this out until it was too late.

Weeks after that conversation I got my edits back. In the margin, diplomatic Jessica had written, "Actually, the phrase is 'kicking @$$ and taking names.' And it's pretty common, almost to the point of cliché." (Creative spelling, mine.)

When I read Jessica's note, I about wanted to fall into a hole and shrivel up. Dust to dust. Can you imagine? First-time author, some silly girl from California, thinks she can write an actual book! Is she really that dumb? I was imagining my brilliant editor, who has worked on multiple *New York Times* bestsellers, rethinking the project. *Lord, have mercy. What kind of disillusioned, syntactically challenged person am I working with?*

That night, in the safety of my room, while sitting at my writing desk, I confronted Britt about the whole debacle. I sat with my chair turned toward him, staring at his back while he was putting things away in the closet. "What?! You told her what?!" he spat, eyes wild, whirling around to face me across the room. He was incredulous, beyond belief at what I had said to Jessica, and I was mortified, feeling the shame afresh—sweaty armpits and all.

Desperately working to save face, the claws came out. Arms folded, hurt look pasted on, I sprang out of my chair, ready to rumble.

"Well, you told me you made it up! I'd never heard it before, so why wouldn't I believe you?!" I choked, partly on humiliation, partly on the disbelief that this was actually happening to me. Still, the fiasco carried on.

"That's like saying I made up 'God bless America,' or 'Cowboy up,'" he reasoned, shoulders up and hands spread out, still appalled that I could make such an indulgently bogus statement to my editor. "How could you possibly think I was serious?"

Sadly, I was never swallowed up by a hole in the earth, so I was forced to pull up my big-girl panties and talk to Jessica about it. Suffice it to say, despite all my humiliation, we had a good laugh after I explained how and why her author would say something so audacious. And for the next several months over the editing process, I would throw out a new one my man had "invented": "mind the gap," "surfers rule," and the super creative "peace out." In case you're curious, yes, I left the questionably originated phrase in my first book—apparently, you can say "butt" without too much of a scuffle. Shh, don't tell.

Thanks to my editor, I was now not only more worldly-wise about clichés and their origins, but I also had a more meaningful and purposeful book to present to my readers. She made a million cuts, and countless hours of my work are doubled over in pain on the editing-room floor, but it was worth it. There was a good reason for each deleted word, each moving of phrases in order to better fit the whole manuscript. So many edits were necessary to get to the heart of the matter, and it is the same with life. If we are brave enough to face some red slashes, to have it spoken to us in the margins that we should trim a bit here, some there, that we should press into what's most important, then we will have a more purposeful and meaningful experience on earth.

Receiving that manuscript ablaze with red was daunting at first, to say the least. As I went through word by word, I had a choice whether to accept or reject each suggested edit. And, truthfully, I did a lot of both. But each instance called for inspection, reflection, and a decision. Is this in line with my main goal or mission? Does this detract from or add to the message? And is this true to who I am as a person? Am I writing with legit authenticity? What here is superfluous? What is causing my goals to take a hit? And, finally, is it good? Is it true? Is it beautiful?

I needed a bit of courage to go through the formidable scores of edits, but as I dove in and really examined the manuscript in its entirety, the spark of courage caught fire and I ended up loving the editing process. I loved the power it gave me over the mission of my message. I loved the creativity it afforded as I still had freedom to dress my words up or down at whim, using my voice to drive home a meaningful message. I loved the steady buzz of hard and significant work, of receiving correction and encouragement, of owning the experiences I was writing about and what God was doing in me. What began in trepidation resulted in triumph.

The weeks of heaviest editing were spent in Hawaii. Britt and Isaiah were on a surf trip in Indonesia, so I hopped a plane with two-year-old Fifi and stayed with a friend on the North Shore of Oahu (don't hate—it sounds fancy, but really, I was staying in my friend's studio apartment and eating at food trucks while fighting off one-eyed cats and feral chickens). We went to the coffee shop in the morning and fed muffin crumbs to chubby birds while sipping chai lattes and eating chia pudding. We would spend the mornings swimming and playing on the beach, soaking in the Hawaiian sun until lunchtime. After lunch, Fifi went down for a nap while I cracked open my computer and assessed the edit situation. Afternoons were the same: play, play, play, then buckle down and edit after Fifi was down for the night. Weed through the junk, arrange the good, remember to add in what made the journey more memorable, more meaningful. The work was hard, constant, and exhausting, but it was so fruitful.

❄

There are times when life editing is necessary not just to survive the modern world but to actually go deeper in purpose and joy, to effectuate peace and presence. It takes intention, yes, but more so, it takes courage. It's more than just sorting the mail, deleting the app, opting out of the team bake sale. It's opening your heart to see what God is trying to show you at any given time about the work that needs doing in your life. This might look different for you in different seasons. Sometimes it looks like leaning into prayer; sometimes it looks like journaling. Sometimes it's listening carefully to the loving words of a friend or reading the pages of a book with ears open to what God may be speaking through it.

However it ends up looking, I really believe quiet is the best place to start. If we never sit in quiet, the noise from the outside will continue to penetrate, rendering our hearts dazed and unfeeling. Blaise Pascal said, "All of men's miseries derive from man's inability to sit in a quiet room alone." I doubt that's where they *all* come from, but at least I know from this quote that I'm not the only one. Quiet contemplation makes me squirm, but effectively editing one's life takes redirection, getting one's compass back to true north, and it's in the quiet that we have the opportunity to align our intentions with what God has for our lives. Maybe that means asking pointed questions, like, "Does this habit or opportunity align with God's love for me? Is it in line with God's love for the people who surround me?" or, "Where will this habit or decision eventually lead? Is this for my and my people's good?" And, "What is most important in this very moment?"

When I slow down and ask these questions in the quiet, it helps me look at the big picture of my story, what I'd like the finished product to resemble. For example, I've been married twenty-one years, and I'd like to be married another fifty. So, I ask, will this decision sow peace into my marriage? I'd also like to launch my kids into this world as secure, well-loved, well-taught, spiritually strong humans. Will these habits help me press into that? I'd like to share God's love through word and deed. Does this choice inspire and encourage that? I'd like to work with my hands, making and doing and saying beautiful things that last. Will this habit of being draw me closer to that or away from it? And I'd like to use the body God gave me to keep me moving, to experience God through recreation, through creation, through service. Am I treating it in a way that will help it last?

Looking at life through a macro lens helps us with the micro. And because it's the moments that add up to a life, our edits affect the direction each moment takes. Sowing into deep, healthy, satisfying relationships; sowing into work well done; sowing into true adventure and exploration of God's world; sowing into our surroundings whether new and scary or old and familiar; sowing into our relationship with God, and pressing into the circumstances we find ourselves in the midst of—all these things build upon each other. All bring us to an ultimate destination. It's in the quiet that we ask reflective questions and, by God's grace, see if perhaps we need to refresh our goals or remove what's obstructing them.

✳

In Israel, we found reasons to consider some necessary edits, but one reason that prompted these edits stands out to me as an extraordinary mercy: Jewish holidays. The entire fall season in the Holy Land seemed to be constant holidays. There was weekly Shabbat, the day of rest. There was Rosh Hashanah, Jewish New Year. There was Sukkot, the Feast of Tabernacles. And hurtling right toward the end of our calendar year was Hanukkah. Each of these was steeped in meaning, in the goodness of God, in remembrance of his provision, in celebrating blessing and relationships and peace. But by far the most impactful yet silently holy day to experience was Yom Kippur.

It happened to fall on the day after we were moving out of one rental apartment in Tel Aviv and into another in Zichron Ya'acov. Thankfully, Tal, a sweet Israeli girl we had become friends with, let me know we had to get to our new place early in the day or it wouldn't be possible until the holiday ended the following evening. Since Yom Kippur is the highest holy day for the Jews, the whole country respected the holiday and shut down completely in honor of it. No Jew would be driving, whether secular or religious; in fact, no one would be driving at all on the roads—Jews, Muslims, and Gentiles alike. The highway would be absolutely off-limits.

Grateful for the tip, we got to our new place early enough and, after unloading our things, set out to experience something unexpectedly ethereal. All around the streets we saw Jewish families dressed in white, slowly moving in the same direction. The generations walked together. The silver-haired and slightly stooped walked with the curious and lively youth. The young mothers with gentle, musical voices holding hands with small children, the quietly content empty nesters—all moved together toward a common place, a common goal. Slowly they ambled toward the synagogue, reverently speaking to each other in hushed tones. It reminded me of the elves of Rivendell filing through the forest on the way to sail to the Undying Lands in *The Lord of the Rings*. These contemplative and reverent people were about to assess their hearts and be absolved of a year's worth of sins in order to realign themselves with God.

The Day of Atonement. Yom Kippur. The day the Jews fast from eating and come before God in a posture of repentance. The day the Jews anticipate forgiveness, a day to start over. The day to examine the self, to be made aware of where one has gone awry, to make necessary edits. The day is marked by prayer, the singing of psalms, and welcoming the redline slashes through what needs to be let go. The introspection and correction might hurt a bit, but Yom Kippur is the solemn predecessor to a day of great joy, a day of feasting and celebration for the forgiveness of sins and an about-face turn.

Yom Kippur represents a clean slate, a chance to start over. The solemn hush we experienced while we watched it unfold held an undercurrent of joy, of expectation. The holy day invited engagement from these beloved people of God, acceptance of correction and the maturation to put it into practice. It required humility and submission, but it yielded great joy. That day felt surreal to us, as we in our everyday clothes watched these white-clad people, preparing to undergo transformation, pass before our eyes. It wasn't a thing to be feared, this examination of the heart, but rather a thing to look forward to.

The day of purification is a lot like editing, whether it's books, life, or relationships. It's the engagement, the introspection. It's the humility to see where we have mistakenly bought into what's taking us in a wrong direction, and then trading that for what gets us back on track. It's the confidence of a better result after the slashing red. It's the acceptance, the correction. But mostly it's the encouragement. We get a do-over; we get the fresh and invigorating feeling of letting go. And we get the anticipation of good things to come.

Letting go is often the hardest part. We can be made aware of what's holding us back from the fullness of real life, but it's another thing to pry it out of our stiff little fingers. We don't want to give up the things we think we can't live without. The little habits or beliefs or ways of being that we have become addicted to that numb us to reality. The things we have convinced ourselves help us navigate this world, yet in truth handicap us. And letting go of these things takes trusting that we have an Editor who has our best in mind. As believers in Jesus, this glorious atonement lasts all year long. Grace has been lavished on us, so we live in that gorgeous place, the place between the redlines of correction and the gift of revision. We don't have to wait for Yom Kippur.

Both the peace and purification offered are received from a place of self-examination. Which things am I holding on to because of pride or fear or selfishness? What's holding me back from pressing into my current circumstances? What attitudes do I have that are keeping me from the deep stuff of today? What is stopping me from loving hard, from working hard, from playing hard? What has become addiction that's choking out real life? Asking the questions of what needs to go takes humility and submission, but after that comes the part that takes courage: the red slash. The necessary edits.

My guess is that we all have stuff to edit out of our lives, and because there is strength in the "me too," I'll go first. I've already talked about some of my first-round edits, things I have cut out of my life or that I have to consistently revisit season to season: social media, over-commitment, tech distractions. They're just a smattering of the most obvious things that get me to tune out of the life in front of me and into a fabricated world of drama and chaos, so they are the first to go.

But just like in writing a book, another round of edits calls for the deeper work of a closer look, and it's usually not quite as obvious. Sneaking around in my life's manuscript I've found some destructive habits, attitudes, and choices that need slashing: negative self-talk, shoddy self-care, taking offense easily, believing the worst of people, believing the worst of myself, comparison, self-absorption, emotional distance, fear of intimacy, fear of loss, and debilitating what-ifs. I've seen these things scattered all through me, littering my manuscript and crowding out what's good, but they're surprisingly hard to part with. In a sad, dysfunctional way, I hang on to the negative self-talk as if it can do something for me, as if by pointing out my inner and outer flaws, I can better myself. And I hang on to the what-ifs, dwelling on what's wrong in the world or what's wrong in my relationships, feeding fear rather than feeding love. And I let the sickness of comparison worm its way into my thoughts until I loathe my life.

I want these things gone so the good can shine through. I want to throw off what's hindering me from building a life in which everything is beautiful in its own time.

When I refuse to edit, the thoughts in my head push and jostle and drown out the sweet harmonic voices of grace and love and hope. Yet slashing what crowds out the simple loveliness of real life is always worth the effort. It feels like a loss, but in truth it's pure gain. And while sometimes when we take our redlined junk to the Lord it can feel like walking down death row, it's actually more like the holy hush before the atonement. It's like the people in white, gliding up to the synagogue to meet with the One who loves them: solemn, yet hopeful. And giving up the things that crowd out what's good, true, and beautiful is a loving act toward those who love you. It's cleaning what's smudging our soul windows so that we can better be image bearers of a God of peace and love; it's submitting to the sanctifying work of the Holy Spirit and receiving beauty in return.

Like Mary of Bethany sitting before Jesus, I am fully present and full of peace when I learn to listen to his voice in the middle of the hustle. And like Mary of Bethany pouring out perfume at his feet, when I hear his voice above the accuser, above the critics whether real or imagined, when I hear words of love and joy, I have discovered the better thing. We were made for this. We were made to receive the peace Jesus offers in the atonement and to offer our stories in return to an Editor who has our best story in mind.

We have the invitation of prayer rather than self-reliance. We have the invitation of the Spirit rather than the flesh. Of forgiveness rather than condemnation. Of intimacy rather than distance, of belief rather than distrust. It's the best invitation I've ever gotten. Let's do it.

Let's submit to the Lord and be willing to face the red-lines. Let's engage in the process and write notes in the margins, willing to hear some hard things for the good of the story.

What are the deepest, truest, most beautiful things you want out of life? What is God speaking over you? Have you asked for the courage to leave behind the habits and attitudes and choices that draw you away from peace, rather than toward? It's time to take stock, to listen hard, to make pivotal choices that will mark the rest of your life. It's a time of moving in a holy hush, seeking God's best, listening to what he has to say, then walking in it, pure white. Purification, grace-laden and hopeful.

eleven

QUEEN-SIZE COURAGE

When my kids were little, I never let them watch princess movies. Personally, I harbored serious scorn toward the classic Disney princess story. I mean, what kind of satanic chauvinist makes these things up? There's usually a witch involved, some kind of dysfunctional jealousy over youth and beauty that culminates in trying to murder the princess, and most of the stories end with the princess kissing some random if good-looking (although usually clad in tights) guy she barely just met. Plus, she always has some low-cut trashy outfit on and impossible proportions. Sounds a bit like high school.

But, since "never say never" is the refrain of all parents, by the time our third kid arrived on the scene, I had opened up our world to the occasional princess or two. Not the delicate flower ones, with the eighteen-inch waists and nothing to offer except porcelain beauty and quavering falsettos. I'm talking the ones with strength and grit. Moana learned to sail the South Pacific and confronted a raging lava monster to save her people. Rapunzel was willing to sacrifice her freedom to save a life (although it did happen to be for the hunky guy in tights). And Anna was willing to die for her sister, Elsa, stepping in front of Hans's traitorous sword.

Not all royal girls are merely ribbons, bows, and balls. In fact, many royal women throughout the years have been the embodiment of courage. And not just courage, but pluck in the face of their circumstances, no matter how intimidating. Some princesses are women who know their place in the world and are prepared to run with it.

Let's talk about Esther. The one from the Bible. This is what I know about her: She was a Jew living in exile in the Persian city of Susa. Her parents were both dead, so she was being raised by her cousin Mordecai. She was young, beautiful, and brave. We are told that she was taken to the palace with a throng of other virgins to begin the impossibly licentious parade of beautiful young women through the king's bed—and I thought the Disney princesses had it bad. Esther was caught up in the middle of government-sanctioned human trafficking, finding herself in a strangely opulent and perilous whirlwind without much prior notice. One minute she's sweeping Mordecai's courtyard and side-eyeing the cute boys on their way to Torah school, and the next she's getting powdered and primped so she can jump into bed with a man likely more than twice her age. And, in this situation, "success" would be if she pleased him enough to become the new queen of Persia.

I can't.

Honestly, it's a lot more nightmare than princess story.

As the narrative unfolds, we see the Lord's hand on this lovely and exceptionally valiant young woman. She found favor with the eunuchs in charge, was given custom beauty treatments, a special diet, and the best spot in the harem. That might sound amazing, like a silver lining, but honestly, I'm guessing all she thought for the year leading up to her night with the king was, *Ew.* I mean, let's talk about this: Her whole life as she knew it was gone, bam! Overnight, she was no longer her own, but property of a Persian king. She no longer had her freedom but was kept like a caged animal, only to be let out at her owner's whim. I can't imagine how trapped she must have felt, especially knowing what was coming— but as we find out, Esther was brave. And present. And incredibly fruitful.

Esther's life was not neat or tidy or safe. It was not going as planned, probably not what she dreamed of. It was terrifying at times, even while strangely luxurious at others. But she owned it. She walked into her here and now like a boss. Palace eunuchs with the power to make or break you? Come at me, bro. Royal-style counsel with insider scoop? Sign me up. Strategic friendships and allies? Done and done. Esther was in it to win it. She moved forward in her new life with mettle, accepted wise advice from Hegai, and made a killer impression on the king. She wasn't the kind of girl to mope about her circumstances, and not only did it serve her well, it saved an entire people group from genocide.

We know the rest of the story. Esther not only became queen but gained such favor with the king that, when an evil plot was formed by the wicked Haman, her courage saved the day. She risked her very life to move forward in this radical role God put her in. I'm not going to recount the whole megillah; rather, what I want us to sit with and think about is Esther's courage to invest in her here and now. She absolutely owned her circumstances. When she found herself in the paddy wagon on the first day of the rest of her life in the palace, she could have checked out and not put forth the effort to become queen. Knowing the royal family is subject to treachery and she wouldn't ever be totally safe, she could have slacked off, been purposely not chosen by the king so that she could self-protect. But she chose to opt in. And Esther's choice to opt in not only changed her life—it changed history.

I don't think that a future in a harem with countless beautiful girls doing nothing but lounging and putting on makeup was an option for Esther, so she did her best with what was right in front of her. What's right in front of you right now? Is it a place of position or favor? Is it a place of service or obscurity or difficulty? Is it a place of hard work, of huge responsibility, or is it a place of unfairness? Are you in a tough spot in your marriage? What about with your boss? Have you been put in a place of influence? How about in your personal pain? Your personal triumphs? It's possible, even likely, that diving into our season will prove to be pivotal—it might even make history. Esther inspires me to look for the reality of what's in front of me and to trust that God has put me here "for such a time as this."

There is so much about my current life that doesn't inspire me to opt in. A lot of it is just mundane, mind-numbing, repetitive life—necessary but uninspiring, boring but important. But I've noticed lately that holding me back are some other things with deep roots, and for me, the root is usually fear. Fear of failure, fear of loss, fear of making mistakes, fear of people, fear of judgment, even fear of success. God has been speaking to me in recent weeks about this. Through the Word and journaling and just times sitting in his presence, I have come to realize that I let fear stand in the way of much of what he wants to do through me. It's been my go-to emotion as long as I can remember. The lie goes something like this: *If I curl up right here, if I stay small and don't move, I'll be safe. If I don't try, then I can't fail. If I don't love too much, then I can't lose too much. If I shut out the reality of my here and now, then I won't feel too much if things fall apart. I'm not the only one who has believed the lie; it's been whispered since the beginning of time.*

This lie could have kept Esther from stepping out in trust and saving the Jews; it could have kept the pioneer women of the faith—Mary Magdalene, Mary of Bethany, Mary of Nazareth, Joanna, Lydia, Priscilla, the apostles' wives—from being integral parts of the early church, from spreading the gospel and planting churches and speaking freedom to the captives. The lie could have prevented these women from being used by God where they were, but they didn't let it. God used business women, single women, servants, moms, wealthy, poor, politically connected, obscure. He has a knack for encouraging us to be ourselves while covering us and inspiring us to go at it like it's open season.

When I think of it like that, considering the stories we read of courageous women and all the ways God was with them, I don't know why we have such a hard time with leaning into our real lives. I confessed my fears, but there's more to it. I think we need to ask ourselves why we tend toward a fabricated fictional life rather than the life that is actually ours: Is it the addiction to superficial affirmation? Is it pride or entitlement? Expectations placed on us we can't live up to? Lack of trust? Discontentment? Shortsightedness? Maybe it's a pernicious cocktail of all the above.

Over the past weeks, as I've let God into the tight spaces, the findings have been surprising. I've been making note of what's happening in me when I'm inclined to disengage, and as I'm doing the hard work of letting him in, I'm seeing the parts of myself I've been holding back. What I'm finding is surprisingly simple, surprisingly essential, even: I seem to have forgotten that I am made in the image of God. That he is capable of using my every moment to reflect his glory, to bring life to those around me, to be an integral part of the history of the world.

As I listen to his voice, he exposes the lies that keep

me from going all in. He reveals to me how fear rudely shoves me down, while courage passionately lifts me up. He reveals that fear comes from the enemy while courage comes from God, and that I need to choose who I give ear to accordingly. He's showing me the spaces I need to dive into, the relationships that need cultivation, the ways to use my talents rather than burying them. And that those spaces demand trust: trusting God, trusting other people, trusting myself.

By God's grace, I'm slowly learning to own my current life, my current circumstances. By God's grace I'm encouraged and strengthened to press into motherhood, writing, teaching, community, prayer, friendship, marriage. And he's teaching me to be brave in the sweet times, to quit missing out by self-protecting and waiting for something bad to happen. By God's grace, I can see more plainly the unhealthy places I lean toward, the lies I listen to, and then give my attention to the truth, to the sweet tenderness of Emmanuel. God's tender words move me to embrace truth, authenticity, and to draw courage.

Right in the sweat and tears of the hard work of examining my life and facing my fears, God gave me a picture while I was in prayer. It was a tree, one of those trees you see on the African savannah, silhouetted against a citrus sky. The tree stretched out far, regally bending down, almost touching the earth. Underneath the tree the ground was soft, and there was room to move and run, room even to dance and be free. God is like that tree to me. He is covering me, and yet he gives me clearance to be myself. To dance and run and not be caged in, to be courageous in that freedom because he has covered me. That picture of the tree has taken me through some tough heart issues, and it will take me through more as I grow in faith and wisdom. God is intimately concerned with my life and can be trusted in times of change, in the carefree times, and in the times of heartbreak and disappointment. The picture of the tree beckons me to own my current season, to dive in regardless of the risk, because he is *covering* me, just like he covered Esther. Just like he covers you.

✦

Maybe, like me, you're thinking you could never measure up to Esther, that you have too many issues and too much baggage and it's holding you back from the kind of courage and presence she seemed to walk in so effortlessly. Don't think, though, that it was any easier for her, because she was only human too. Let's go back to Esther's story and see what might have made her want to curl up and check out.

When Haman's evil plot to destroy the Jews was made known to Esther, she found herself in a quandary. Mordecai had been urging her to plead with the king on behalf of their people, yet Esther argued back with all the impossibilities of the situation: no one in the kingdom was allowed to go before the king without being invited first on threat of death, and it had been thirty days since the king had called for her anyway. Mordecai reminded her with this famous yet chilling truth: "Don't think for a moment that because you're in the palace you will escape when all the other Jews are killed. If you keep quiet at a time like this, deliverance and relief for the Jews will arise from some other place, but you and your relatives will die. Who knows if perhaps you were made queen for just such a time as this?" (Esther 4:13–14).

This time, Esther found herself not in the middle of a royal beauty pageant but in the very crux of the threat of genocide. The battle was raging in and around her, and the misgivings and fear and lies would have been her daily companions. Perhaps she struggled with the lie that God didn't love her because her life had been turned upside down. Or the lie that she had no voice in her current situation—just as she hadn't when she was just one of many women in the harem—and could never truly make a difference. That she was only made up of her outer beauty. That God was not listening, so why bother to pray. That it would be suicide to confront the king, that the flavor was wearing off and she wasn't quite so palatable anymore. That he probably wouldn't change his mind about demolishing the Jews anyway, so just stay in your lane, little girl. The urge to withdraw must have been overwhelming, yet Mordecai's sage words held weight.

Instead of giving in to the lies and fears she must have had, Esther put away her initial hesitation, made up her mind, and took her situation a step further. Her engagement in the battle began with entering into God's presence; she and her maids fasted for three days. Grabbing those who were in her sphere of influence, those who God put around her at that season of her life, she faced her situation beginning with prayer. Esther didn't check out; she jumped right in. She was fully present. She was brave. And she was fruitful. And I believe it came from trusting God, from inviting his presence into her circumstances rather than running from them.

We all have something useful, lovely, and even powerful to bring to the table. Esther happened to use her beauty and wisdom for good, but not many of us are currently wearing a crown. What about the rest of us? What can we bring to the table right where we are, in our current season? We are all equipped to make a difference when we opt in; we are all being called to right now. Those callings look as unique and individual as each one of us: being women in leadership, working for NGOs, running businesses, doing creative work, raising children, women who make beautiful things or women who stay behind the scenes. And we do it as single women, married women, widows, and mamas. This all happens as we utilize our God-given individual strengths and step intentionally into the spaces and places where God has given us influence.

But when I see so few of us step up to the plate, I realize there's something insidious that's killing our potential: comparison. Comparison is a cousin to that fear we've been talking about. When we go around constantly comparing ourselves with each other, looking at everyone else's life, we begin fearing we're not good enough and start hating our own talents and lives. We see what others are doing and feel small, insignificant.

Think of all the voices we've heard over our lifetimes: voices of judgment, discontentment, voices rendering us useless. It starts when we're young, when we are told that we need to be someone else, someone more, to be happy. That who we are isn't good enough. We are told we should have had someone else's talent, looks, or career. We hear it so often we start to believe the voices. We wonder, *How did I get stuck in the wrong peer group, the wrong school? In the wrong career or with the wrong husband or in the wrong city?* Seldom do we look around, whether at the mess or the glory, and say, "Yes, this is my real, tangible life, and I'm in. This is my actual career, these are my actual kids, this is my actual community/dress size/zip code/passion/sphere of influence, and I am all in, whether it's boring or beautiful, whether painful or propitious."

When do we stop pining for someone else's life and own ours? When do we look around at our people, our social status, our giftings, and say, "Yes! Bring it on, Lord. How will you use me here? How will you show yourself as I invest in this season, this moment? How will I be changed or promote change? How can I love well? What will you teach me? How will you open my eyes to what I have, not what I lack? How will I experience your goodness?"

I'm as guilty as anyone else on this matter. I've been wishing for what other people have since I was in junior high. I can remember wanting someone else's looks, talent, or boyfriend. When I was pregnant, working full-time, and taking twenty units so I could graduate college before my son was born, I wished for someone else's schedule, someone else's freedom. When my babies were young and spitting up everywhere and laundry piled up to the roof, I wished for someone else's life stage. As a pastor's wife I've wished for someone else's elbow room, someone else's liberty and anonymity. But what have I been missing? What is God doing with me right now that I'm not willing to see? What does he want to do in my life if only I would pick up my pink gel pen and check yes?

More and more I hear stories of women who rise to the occasion right where they are. They have chosen not to hide or check out but to lean in and be brave. Women surviving human trafficking who have risen out of the ashes to help other women in the same situation. Stay-at-home moms humbly serving their families, creating an atmosphere of love, and supporting children who grow strong and rise up to serve others. I know single women who choose not to pine after a man in order to live well, but who instead live boldly, traveling and serving and making history. There are also poor women, experiencing the nearness of God as provider, constantly sharing God's goodness with their communities. There are wealthy women, embracing the responsibility God has placed on them, using their means to share his love. I know widows who are brokenhearted, yet in their pain are bold in their season of sorrow, asking how God will show himself to them and in them.

You get the picture. The table is full. It's full and lively and altogether powerful. And so, so beautiful.

Our circumstances and seasons are ours alone, whether uncomfortable, painful, and lonely, or abundant, easy, and even extravagant. No matter which we are in, they are not to be disregarded, not to be considered a mistake. They are meaningful, whether they are hard times or good ones. They are individual and important. There is a time for everything, yes, and everything is beautiful in its time. And yet, we don't see the whole scope of God's work from beginning to end.

When Isaiah was three years old and Daisy was a baby, I was trying to figure out what to do with my life. I hadn't thought much beforehand about what I would do when children joined our family, so I had no expectations. We had just planted our church, and I thought I might go into women's ministry and focus my time with our church baby, as all I could see were women in need of discipleship and encouragement. My seasons had changed, going from a single girl to married with two young children in just a few years' time, and I was just feeling it all out. I don't remember whether I asked her or not, but a dear friend of ours—a pillar and spiritual mother of our church—shared something with me that had the power to change my family for good.

She told me and Britt that she felt like the Lord was saying I was to spend the heart and core of myself on my young children and not go to work at that time. She said God was showing her something was going to happen in Isaiah's life when he was around nine years old, and he would be desperate for everything I had to pour out to him. Despite the needs I saw at church, this rang true with me, and I gave myself to my kids, staying home with them and leaning into that season. It wasn't always idyllic; those days with babies and preschoolers were long and messy and tedious. They seemed hidden from view and thankless and unproductive. I couldn't see the whole scope of God's work; I could only lean in close and opt in right where I was. But now, looking back, I see the hand of God was all over us.

Isaiah was nine when his sister was diagnosed with cancer.

He needed every moment I gave him: every prayer, every song, every story. Every beach day, every sandwich, every art project. And when I think back to those long lonely days, I see the loveliness sprinkled all through them. The peanut butter kisses. The water balloon fights.

The neck hugs, the lisp, the discipline, the ice cream cones, the dropping of everything to kiss a skinned knee. We both needed those years, especially in light of what our next season of cancer treatment and being uprooted in Israel and losing Daisy brought.

Thank God our friend was willing to share what the Lord was showing her with courage, and thank God he equipped me for such a time as that. It makes me think of how our seasons flow, interconnected, not only in our own lives but in the lives of those around us. We each have something important to give, to receive, to walk in, no matter what season we find ourselves in the middle of. It could be a time of sowing into our young children or a time of self-sacrifice for family. Maybe a time of loss. It could be a time of growth, of learning and equipping, whether in school or an apprenticeship. Each season has its sweet times and its bitter ones, and we are guaranteed there will always be another season we'd rather be in. But God, making everything beautiful in its own time, is working in and through each of us. And like Esther, we'd do well to have the courage to see that and partner with him.

Even right now, in a house with a homeschooled teenager, with a wild three-year-old, with a writing career and a beautiful church and friends who make my heart sing, I am conscious of wishing I could push the fast-forward button on different parts of my current life. Even right now, daily, I sit with Jesus and pour it all out—the hurts, fears, jealousies, insecurities. And even right now, without a crown yet offering the courage of a queen, he bends down and says, "I have equipped you for such a time as this." And he's saying it to you too.

twelve

VALUABLE SOUVENIRS

Coming home from Israel was an adventure in and of itself. While we were there, the weather had begun to turn. The sky transformed from the archetypal Middle Eastern autumn pale beige, barely discernable from the arid landscape, to a sweet, crisp, brilliant blue. Our last few weeks there felt different in every way. The Mediterranean was no longer inviting without a wetsuit, there was no swell to speak of, and the chill in the air was undeniable. The parched earth's cry for water was finally heard by heaven, and so began the heaviest rainstorms I've ever experienced.

A particularly angry squall was raging in the night as we left the country. The lightning streaked across the sky just like in the movies, and the thunder rattled my bones. At 4:00 a.m. we had crammed all our luggage into our tiny tin can of a car and strapped our surfboards on top. We dashed through the inky darkness toward the open doors, bringing in as much rain as we kept out. Lightning lit up the empty highway, giving it an eerie feel. The fat drops crashing onto the roof created a rushing, deafening hypnotic sound. And to make it that much more of a hostile situation, the straps that held the boards down broke the rubber seals of our car windows, and rain coursed down through the woven nylon and poured onto our knees in thin icy rivulets.

We sat in the car in silence as we drove the hour and a half to Ben Gurion Airport. The rush to get on the road had settled, and each of our minds privately contemplated the past three months. We thought about our last morning in Israel: pitch black, clapping thunder, wet, cold. We thought about the country we had learned to navigate, which no longer seemed foreign, the ways we had all changed, the things we'd seen and discovered and become. We wondered what would come next for our little family. What ways of being would we bring home with us? There had been so much to learn, so much to soak in. Such an exit seemed monumental.

We stopped in Boston on the way back to California, and as soon as we got out to the international flight arrival zone, Britt collapsed his six-foot-six-inch frame all the way down and kissed the actual floor—right there among the boisterous shouts of reunited families, the lingering embraces of lovers, the limo drivers with their misspelled signs. Despite all we had gained on our trip, a big part of us wanted to shake the dust from the whole experience—the traffic, the litter, the cultural brusqueness, the honking, the loneliness and emotional struggle, and the physical pain of Daisy's treatments. Our first inclination was to go back to the way things were before we went to Israel, not wanting to admit any good had come from our taxing experience. But, ultimately, we couldn't deny the beauty of the way we had learned to do life, and we discovered that our lessons, experiences, and memories were the most valuable of souvenirs. Being in Boston was somewhat of a buffer, a grace period of neither here nor there. But real life was coming—our real home, our real jobs, our real relationships. I hoped we had packed our emotional bags accordingly.

After just a couple of weeks back home, we ended up in the hospital again with Daisy's fourth and final diagnosis. We spent all of December right back where we had been before we left for Israel: in a hospital bed, depressed and staring out the window at concrete walls. Only this time it was much worse. Cancer is a dirty schoolyard bully, and she beat my girl up right in front of my eyes. Living through the last two months of Daisy's life crushed my soul to dust, and when her body gave out, we knew nothing could ever be the same. We just couldn't go back to the way things were—life was too precious for that.

※

Pivotal moments pave the way for pivotal choices. And Daisy's death was one more pivotal moment in our crazy flow. I not only changed my email address and stayed off social media but went completely dark on the blog as well. It appeared that going off the grid was not only to be for our overseas health emergency, but for as long as it took to grieve, as long as it took to get our breath back.

Presence took on a whole new meaning, and our friendships and family ties were more precious than ever. Our withdrawal was considered radical by many, so to communicate why we would choose that lifestyle, Britt sent this email out to everyone at our church:

Dear friends,

The last few years have been most difficult for my family and me. Among other challenging things, my eight-year-old daughter Daisy Love died on February 16, 2013. Our three-and-a-half-year battle with cancer was happening during a time of expansion in the ministry of Reality with our church plants in San Francisco and Boston and campus launch in Santa Barbara. All of this left us quite exhausted, and when Daisy was diagnosed with cancer for the third time on Easter week of 2012, the elders granted me an indefinite leave of absence to take care of myself and family.

Late that summer we went to Israel for three months to seek experimental cancer treatment for Daisy. Just prior to and during that time, the Lord was speaking to our family about living a different way. About being less connected to technology and the rest of world and more present to God and each other. In Israel, we went off the grid, so to speak, and left behind our phones and internet connections and social media and the like. We were discovering what, for us, was a better way of being. Living in the moment and not worrying about posting updates, returning phone calls and emails, checking in on the rest of the world, and constantly being entertained. Instead we gave each other and God our full attention. We played games as a family, took long walks, relaxed, played more, and prayed more. Our kids, Isaiah and Daisy, were so thankful to always have our full attention and not compete with iPhones and text messages, and Kate and I were so happy to be present to each other and God in a brand-new way. And though it was challenging at times, we relished the isolation and obscurity that living disconnected in the Middle East afforded us.

When we came home from Israel we knew things could not be exactly the same, as we would happily reconnect with friends and family and I would return to the ministry at Reality. But we also knew that things could not be the way they were before with the constant connectivity of technology and the way it removed us from being present with those around us and with what we are doing. We have been trying to chart a course that is both faithful to the ministry the Lord has entrusted us with and faithful to the more present, less-connected way of being he has been teaching us. It has not always been easy, and there is much to it. I have a flip phone that does not get text messages or go online. We have no internet connection at our house. We are not on social media. There are tweaks and things to figure out along the way, but it is going well and has been life-giving.

Part of what God has been teaching us in being

present is to live more simply, to live smaller and faithfully with those he has put us near. For me, with the platform I have had, that means being willing to decrease and embrace obscurity and crucify ego. Also, the Lord has given me a fresh love, devotion, passion, and focus for the local church I am a part of. My goal is to be faithful to my local church and the community, and for me to do that, I have to be solely concerned with living with and preaching to them and not others. This is where my sermons no longer being online comes into play. My sermons will only be made available online to those who attend our local church who will have access through our website via a login password they received at church. I apologize if this upsets anyone who has enjoyed or been helped by my preaching ministry over the years, but this is what I need to do within the limits and joys of my own weaknesses to be faithful in being present where I am.

Love,

Britt

It was a new day, a new season. It was a chance to push the reset button and jump into today, however that looked in work or community, relationships or Sabbath. With our Israeli experience behind us and our new normal in front of us, we needed to leave room for adjustment. We left room to take it slow, to keep our notifications off, to allow life to be savored, not drunk from like a fire hose.

The souvenirs of that time served me well, even the silly ones. I still get emails in my inbox from two places that I've never unsubscribed from: Kosher Gift Baskets and Torah Educational Software. Somehow, creepily so, while we were in Israel we started getting these solicitations. But the funny thing is, I like getting them. I get about one a week, and every time I see one it reminds me of our adventure in the Holy Land, of solitude and listening and Sabbath and with-ness. It reminds me that life is fragile, that people are important. It takes me back to the holy holidays we observed, to the ancient ruins we explored, to the Garden of Gethsemane and the God-Man who sweated drops of blood. Those emails murmur, *Nothing's changed since then. Life is still just as lovely and brutal and precarious. Your moments are every bit as valuable today as they ever were.*

❋

These days, eight years after kicking the Sephora box, life is so different. I'm stunned at what I see when I look back. I survived living in a foreign land under desperate circumstances. I survived caring for my Daisy girl. I survived giving her over to God. And I survived the subsequent grief. I feel like a different person in so many ways, new layers I've put on, new memories, skills, and wisdom. Gosh, I've lived a lot of life so far. When I back up even further, I see an even more radical picture of what God has done in and through me. My past twenty years of being a grown-up—of ministry, career, family, survival, love, death, loss, and spiritual breakthrough— were nothing like I had expected. It wasn't the script I had written for myself. In many ways, those things were so much harder than anything I thought was possible, yet I see that each season of life meant something. Each was purposeful. And each had opportunity to be fruitful, to yield buckets and buckets of shiny plump fruit.

The Teacher in Ecclesiastes knew what he was talking about. I could not possibly have seen the whole scope of God's work from beginning to end, that much was true. But even in the darkest hour, there was beauty and light. It's like God was lovingly nudging me. *One step at a time, lovely girl. That's it, now another. Just hold my hand, and when we climb to the top you'll see it all laid out.* It's something to release control of life—flying free, no parachute, no net. And even after everything I've been through, this passage is a balm to my heart as I write, and I hope it is for you too: "God has made everything beautiful for its own time. He has planted eternity in the human heart, but even so, people cannot see the whole scope of God's work from beginning to end" (3:11).

Let go. He's got me. He's got you.

The Sephora box gave me a little perspective. It gave me a tangible, cube-shaped, cardboard reminder of what real life is. You know, I had plans for my life before that fateful day. And caring for a dying girl wasn't one of them.

But God handed me just that. I realize now that caring for a precious and suffering girl was, in fact, my real life. That it was meaningful, prayerful, powerful, beautiful. Every gentle word spoken, every story whispered, every tear dried, every thermometer swipe was my real life.

So much of the time, when the life we want gets interrupted, we tend to see it as a diversion. A wrench in our plans, a waste of time. We see the interruptions as unfortunate and exasperating and dull. But I have learned that God says differently. Bumps in the road aren't a diversion from real life; they *are* real life. Children don't keep you from your real life; children *are* real life. Aging parents are real life. Education and exploration and employment are all real life. Feeding your loved ones. That's real life. Caring for your community. That's real life. Worship, prayer, communion. That's real life. And while we may have had dreams or expectations otherwise, those things would be the exception and not the rule.

Let's enter into the real life of right here, right now. What does your today look like? What have you been seeing as a diversion? What are you antsy about and eager to be past so you can get to the important stuff? What are the expectations you hold on to that don't leave room for small, ordinary moments? Are you nurturing a fledgling relationship or mending an old one? Are you elbow-deep in washing cloth diapers? Are you in the space of gathering those around you? Are you in a space of growth, or creativity, or change? How about the pain of getting free from addiction? The pain of loss? God has made everything beautiful in its time, and times have a habit of changing—so look for what's beautiful right now.

✳

I look back at myself at different ages, different stages, and I want to tell my past selves so much. Here, on the other side, with all the grace and all the love God has given me, I want to tell my sixteen-year-old self she is worth more than she knows. More than the piercing voices telling her otherwise. That she has a delightful future of love and respect coming, that she would do well to wait for it. I want to tell her, "Be your crazy self. Don't let others define who you are, and, for the love, choose some better friends. Even so, God will use these days."

I want to tell my twenty-year-old self that she has a future of creative, meaningful work. That she has gifts she hasn't discovered yet, gifts that are latent, having been tucked into the quiet places, waiting to see the light. I want to tell her to be free in her education, to run with what she loves, what she's gifted with, rather than choosing the safer, less passionate areas of study. I want to tell her that it's okay to like that children's literature class best and not to forget to take more art classes! "God will use these days."

I want to tell my twenty-three-year-old self that God will do more in his kingdom than she can imagine, that obedience now in college ministry will blossom into something wonderful only God has the power to accomplish. I want to tell her, "Yes, keep picking up trash at midnight after college gatherings while eight months pregnant. Yes, keep providing a safe place for girls to laugh and cry. Keep hosting sleepovers and cooking huge pots of beans; keep listening and giving it straight. Those relationships are golden. They are long-lasting. So invest. And, please, take your leaders camping more often! God will use these days."

I want to tell my twenty-six-year-old self, "Yes, you will sleep again, even though a tiny human has taken over your world." And, "No, your body will never be the same, so just choose to love it, because it has been a vehicle for the miracle of life. And even though your boobs look like bloodshot eyeballs and you feel like a dairy cow, they will go back to normal in time." I want to tell her to pour out and pour out and pour out, with joy and spirit, because the investment in this little life will return dividends. "God will use these days."

I want to tell my thirty-year-old self that the child and church that were birthed right after each other will both stab her heart and make her proud. I want to say, "You aren't worthy of either, but that's the beauty. Yes, keep trusting God with your gifts, and know that even though things will never stay the same with either your baby girl or your baby church, God has you in his right hand. This is all part of the grand story. He can be trusted with these fragile and precious things. God will use these days."

I want to tell my thirty-four-year-old self, "Yes, this is heinous, this awful cancer diagnosis." And, "You are ultimately not in control, but God is." I want to say, "Honey, sweet, sweet mama, you've got to trust God. Worrying only gives you ulcers and makes everyone around you anxious." I want to say, "God has equipped you for this season. He has made you strong. Walk in it. Chin high, shoulders back. And fight for what's important. Fight for connection, privacy, wisdom, for your son who is thrown in the middle of the crisis. These moments are full of wonder and wretchedness. God will use these days."

I want to tell my thirty-eight-year-old self that the sun will shine again. That even though Daisy is gone, she will rise in the grace and goodness of a loving Father. That it's okay to take as much time as she needs, that tears feel really, really good, so let them flow. I want to tell her to have the courage to face her grief, to journal more, to check out less. And that bitterness isn't a viable way of life. I want to tell her God won't waste her pain, that he will bring beauty for ashes. "God will use these days."

I want to tell all my past selves to march on, that it's the small things of right now that make up the landscape of a life. That there will be love and victory and trials. That there will be miracles and heartache, that there will be reason and purpose. I want to tell them, "God sees the whole scope of his work in your life, but you're only responsible for right now, this very minute, and that is a huge relief."

And here I sit, barely forty-three, in a new season of life with a seventeen-year-old son and a three-year-old daughter, and a family of churches that has grown across both the Atlantic and the Pacific. I think I would ask my future self, "How do I stay the course in motherhood? How can I send my man-child off into the world in only a year? Will the piece of my heart he takes with him ever stop bleeding? How will I survive the preschool years with Fifi? Will I ever get to go to the bathroom in private? And do I really have to live here on this broken earth for another forty years?"

I think I know what she'd say to me. I think I'm seeing a pattern. What would she say ten years from now? How about ten months from now? She knows how it plays out by then, the things I get to experience, the resulting outcome of my worries. Would she hold me and whisper encouragement? Would she say, "Things are sweet right now; don't waste it"? Would she give me a list of to-dos or tell me to pull up my big-girl panties? Would she tell me to take a vacay? Would she shout, "Toe the line, woman! Stand firm!"?

A woman I've never met who lost her son to leukemia a few years before I lost Daisy once emailed me an encouragement. In that precious note, she said, "Today is all you have; it's all anyone has." That simple crumb of wisdom brought me considerable relief. It still does. I'm only responsible for today. In a world of tomorrows, of full calendars and a hundred ways to worry, that short and shrewd sentence is permission for presence.

Wherever you are, right now, give it your whole self. Don't think about yesterday and all you should've done differently. Don't think about tomorrow and how it will all come together. Don't miss today. This moment. This moment and the next and the next make up a life. How we choose to spend them makes up the next ten minutes, the next ten months, the next ten years. This moment, strung like pearls with all the other moments, will make history, your history. My history. A history marked by courage. By presence. By fruitfulness.

We are here, now. And I know I am in the right place. Because today we listen to the rain come down on the metal roof. Fifi skateboards in the living room and stops to ask me to smell her lips, and I gladly oblige. Today the dishes pile up, and the manuscript is finished. The husband is killing weeds, and the son is taking photos outside. This moment will melt into the next. This moment will sow into the future. This moment is beautiful, will be beautiful, because I'm right where I'm supposed to be.

ACKNOWLEDGMENTS

I t's been said that writing a book is a lot like having a baby. From conception to birth there are others involved—it's not a one-woman show. From knitting together all the parts of the body to the care and health of the message to bringing to light a prize you finally hold in your hands, it was not created by itself, nor will just one person enjoy it. I have the loveliest team of support around me: friends, editors, family, and readers. You all played a crucial part in birthing this book and I couldn't have done it without you.

First and foremost, thank you Jesus for being the best, most impactful example of presence to me. Your short life was so beautiful, so filled with meaning and strength and kindness in the healings and in the heartbreak. I only wish I was there to witness the looks on the faces of those you spent time with, wish I could've seen your body language convey unspoken love. Thank you for showing me the way of true love and how to choose the better thing.

To Britt. You actually, literally complete me. Thank you for being the best freaking husband and dad on the planet. Thank you for being cosmic with me and encouraging me to go after what's life giving; from surfing to keeping horses and raising chickens to writing books to dancing on the patio table. Life without you would absolutely rot. You are a total gift to the world, and I get to enjoy you the most.

To Jessica, my editor, you teased the concept out of me with your pointed questions, probing and pressing until enough life was sparked to take root. Thank you for doing your job with excellence. I am privileged to have worked with you twice now—your quiet and firm stance for good writing is a gift. Thank you for making me rewrite the manuscript, and don't worry, I'll forgive you for only giving me thirty days to do it. I appreciate you, plus I really like you.

To Don Jacobson, my friend, agent, and encourager. Thank you for loving my family, for allowing us to love yours. Thank you for shooting straight, for making me feel like a real author way before I ever was published. You are a gift to the Merricks!

To my girls at Nelson Books: Brigitta, Sara, and Aryn. Thank you for rolling with my constant blooper reel, for taking care of business like total bosses, for loving books, and for making me feel at ease in all the extra book-y things you never realize you'll have to do. I'm so lucky to get to work with you girls a second time! You three are accomplished and helpful and full of grace.

To all the precious people and organizations who gave so that we could go to Israel and seek healing. Your contribution may not have saved Daisy's life, but I'm pretty sure it saved mine. Thank you for your generosity to a desperate family. Hopefully some of what I discovered there can now benefit you.

To my family and Britt's family, you have brought us up to enjoy the most beautiful and wild things in life. Thank you for making sure we learned how to fish and surf and bake from scratch and keep a garden and appreciate the invaluable things in life. Thank you to both our moms for making us go outside and play. Jesus was waiting for us out there.

Isaiah, you are the raddest kid I can ever imagine being a mom to. Thank you for climbing every rock in Israel, for surfing with us and playing cards in every café and letting me draw a face on your chin and make videos of you singing. Thank you for loving your sister so fiercely. We couldn't have done it without you.

Daisy, you were the most joyful, brave, confident, creative little scamp. Our friends in Israel are better for having met you. Thank you for letting us video you lip syncing to *Tel-Aviv'n* and singing Shabbat Shalom. You are a treasure and I can't wait to see you again.

Fifi, thank you for keeping it real in the Merrick household. For terrorizing your brother, dressing Dad up in your bunny ears and princess jewelry, and kicking the snuggle factor way up. You are positively full of sunshine.

Thank you for the way you tell me you miss your sister, I know she misses you too.

To the Abdulla family, stopping in Boston both while leaving the country and returning was a privilege and gift. It gave us courage to fly and again for reentry. Thank you for being true friends to us, for all our bare honesty with each other, for dancing in the kitchen to 80s music, and for loving us like family.

To Jamie, thank you for being positively fabulous and writing the most butt-kicking foreword a girl could ask for! Your encouragement and friendship mean so much to me, from the three hours we spent under the blinking lights at Lambert's to enjoying Spritz in the Italian countryside, you've been a true encourager, a solid truthteller, and make me want to follow hard after Jesus. Plus, you have a heart the size of Texas.

And to all my endorsers, thank you for being examples of people who rise to the occasion and make a beautiful life, right where you are. Each of you inspires me, and I'm proud to have your name on my book.

ABOUT THE AUTHOR

K ate writes, speaks, helps plant churches, and loves
talking about how great Jesus is. She also special-
izes in making up dances to *The Greatest Showman*
soundtrack, riding a surfboard, horse, or roller skates,
and adding more butter to pretty much everything. She
lives in Carpinteria, California, with her family and some
fluffy chickens.

To find more of Daisy's story and watch her memo-
rial, visit Kate's blog at kmerrick.com/daisy/. To read
about Kate's journey after losing Daisy and moving from
bitterness to joy, read *And Still She Laughs: Defiant Joy in
the Depths of Suffering*.